THE
COMPLI
IDIOT'S
GUIDE® TO

Customizing Your Ride

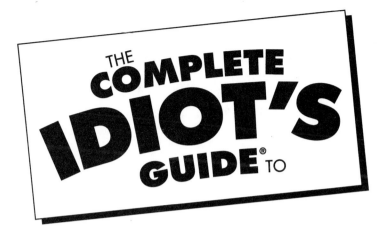

THE COMPLETE IDIOT'S GUIDE® TO

Customizing Your Ride

by Tom Benford with Andy Goodman

ALPHA

A member of Penguin Group (USA) Inc.

Tom's Dedication:

Yet another book for you, Liz, the love of my life, my wife, soul mate and best friend!

Andy's Dedication:

Follow your dreams as persistence will prevail! Thank you, Valerie, for following them with me!

ALPHA BOOKS

Published by the Penguin Group

Penguin Group (USA) Inc., 375 Hudson Street, New York, New York 10014, USA

Penguin Group (Canada), 90 Eglinton Avenue East, Suite 700, Toronto, Ontario M4P 2Y3, Canada (a division of Pearson Penguin Canada Inc.)

Penguin Books Ltd., 80 Strand, London WC2R 0RL, England

Penguin Ireland, 25 St. Stephen's Green, Dublin 2, Ireland (a division of Penguin Books Ltd.)

Penguin Group (Australia), 250 Camberwell Road, Camberwell, Victoria 3124, Australia (a division of Pearson Australia Group Pty. Ltd.)

Penguin Books India Pvt. Ltd., 11 Community Centre, Panchsheel Park, New Delhi—110 017, India

Penguin Group (NZ), 67 Apollo Drive, Rosedale, North Shore, Auckland 1311, New Zealand (a division of Pearson New Zealand Ltd.)

Penguin Books (South Africa) (Pty.) Ltd., 24 Sturdee Avenue, Rosebank, Johannesburg 2196, South Africa

Penguin Books Ltd., Registered Offices: 80 Strand, London WC2R 0RL, England

Copyright © 2007 by Tom Benford

International Standard Book Number: 978-1-59257-654-8
Library of Congress Catalog Card Number: 2006940261

09 08 07   8 7 6 5 4 3 2 1

Interpretation of the printing code: The rightmost number of the first series of numbers is the year of the book's printing; the rightmost number of the second series of numbers is the number of the book's printing. For example, a printing code of 07-1 shows that the first printing occurred in 2007.

Printed in the United States of America

Note: This publication contains the opinions and ideas of its authors. It is intended to provide helpful and informative material on the subject matter covered. It is sold with the understanding that the authors and publisher are not engaged in rendering professional services in the book. If the reader requires personal assistance or advice, a competent professional should be consulted.

Publisher: *Marie Butler-Knight*
Editorial Director/Acquiring Editor: *Mike Sanders*
Managing Editor: *Billy Fields*
Development Editor: *Ginny Munroe*
Production Editor: *Kayla Dugger*
Copy Editor: *Nancy Wagner*

Cartoonist: *Chris Eliopoulos*
Cover Designer: *Bill Thomas*
Book Designer: *Trina Wurst*
Indexer: *Brad Herriman*
Layout: *Chad Dressler*
Proofreader: *Aaron Black*

Contents at a Glance

Contents

Introduction

Welcome to the fun and often outrageous world of modified sport compact cars known as "tuners." As you'll learn on the following pages, modifying sport compact cars (SCCs for short) can go from mild to wild with a lot of steps in between—the only limitations are your imagination and resources.

We discuss different types of modifications you can make to your ride, and these run the gamut from changing the outward appearance of your car to improving power and handling to making interior improvements to installing killer stereo and entertainment systems and much more. And we won't just be discussing it—we'll show and tell you how to do it, too.

In writing this book, we're assuming that you have little or no previous knowledge or experience customizing cars, and that's OK. The approaches we've taken with the various modifications you'll find here don't require an automotive engineering degree or an extensive, well-equipped workshop facility. A lot of desire, the ability to follow directions, and some elbow grease are the main ingredients you'll need to do the vast majority of these modifications.

A lot of the customizations we're covering here are "bolt-on" modifications that, to a large extent, consist of removing one component and replacing it with another. You will find some projects that are a bit more involved and require some specific tools and skill. For these projects you may decide to undertake them yourself or perhaps enlist outside help—that will be your call.

Our overall objective here is to help you customize your ride to make it what you want it to be. In the final analysis, making your ride the unique expression of your particular vision, aspiration, and taste is really what customizing is all about. We encourage you to go for it, and we'll help you to do so.

How to Use This Book

The Complete Idiot's Guide to Customizing Your Ride segregates the art and craft of customizing into distinct parts that focus on the various aspects associated with it. Here's a breakdown of what's covered in each of the seven parts.

Part 1, "The Fast-Paced World of Tuners," introduces you to the sport compact car phenomenon and how it got started, the major manufacturers and different body types of SCCS, the process of turning a stock SCC into a tuner, reasons for customizing your ride, and exploring your various options.

Part 2, "Getting Started," here you assess your current ride, deciding what you want to do to it, defining what's legal and what isn't, creating a budget for your time and money, allocating a work space, figuring out tool requirements, assessing your own skill levels and the labor that will be needed, creating a project plan, and addressing safety concerns.

Part 3, "Outward Appearances," is devoted to customizing the exterior of your ride. Things such as front and rear lighting, grilles, lip and body kits, hoods, deck lids, fenders, doors, paint and graphics, and window treatments are all covered herein.

Part 4, "Performance—Packing More Ponies," is all about increasing the horse-power of your ride. It covers such topics as intake, exhaust, ignition, computers, fuel, nitrous, and boosted induction.

Part 5, "Hit the Road," directs attention to brakes, shocks, springs, coilovers, air and hydraulic suspension systems, struts and sway bars, calipers, discs and pads for better stopping, and wheels and tires.

Part 6, "Customizing the Cabin," takes you inside the car and focuses on custom knobs, pedals, handles, gauges, seating and upholstery options, neon and LED accent lighting, and audio/video equipment for your ride.

Part 7, "Car Culture," explores SCC and tuner clubs, cruise nights, car shows, sponsors, runs, and events, and even getting your car in the movies or on TV commercials. We also discuss taking your ride to the track to see what she can do, what you'll need, what to expect, required safety gear, and what's involved for more serious racing endeavors.

Extras

Throughout *The Complete Idiot's Guide to Customizing Your Ride*, you'll find little pearls of wisdom and informational gems peppering the pages in little boxes called sidebars. These sidebars will provide you with additional tips, warnings, definitions, and even some interesting trivia facts. Their purpose is to be helpful, to give you some extra information, and even to lighten things up a bit by providing some amusement.

IN THE KNOW

There are lots of little tips, techniques, shortcuts, and advice we've amassed over the years in our experience working with and customizing cars, and we share them with you in these sidebars.

YELLOW FLAG

You'll find words of warning and caution in these sidebars—they're meant to help prevent injuries and save you time and money by alerting you to potential pitfalls and dangers.

TUNER TALK

The tuner world has its own jargon. Here's where you'll find definitions for a lot of the talk you'll hear and use.

TUNER TRIVIA

Obscure, little-known facts and tidbits associated with the entire customizing scene will be found in these sidebars, and you may frequently be surprised and amused by them. Customizing is a fun activity, so the order of the day is to have fun—starting with this book!

Acknowledgments

No book is ever solely the product of its author or authors; such is surely the case with *The Complete Idiot's Guide to Customizing Your Ride*. There are several people who, in various measures, provided their help, assistance, advice, suggestions, products, services, or other important elements that all contributed in some part to helping us create and complete this book. It's only right and fitting that we take a moment to thank those good people here and now:

Liz Benford for her encouragement, organizational support, and scheduling

Valerie Goodman for her patience, understanding, and support

Michael Snell at the Snell Literary Agency

Jim Hegadorn at Fuji Photo Film USA

John Sloane at The Eastwood Company

Mike Yager and Cheryl Habing at Mid America Motorworks

David Reider for his excellent photography

Neil Tjin for "covering Andy's back"

Bob at Camerabits.com

Matt Edmonds at The Tire Rack

Mark Chervany at Goodyear Tire & Rubber

Mike Sanders at Alpha/Penguin

Ginny Bess Munroe at Alpha/Penguin for her excellent editing and good humor

Without a doubt, there were others, some of whom we don't know by name, but their efforts on our behalf are nonetheless worthy of acknowledgment. To everyone who helped us in any capacity, we offer our most sincere and heartfelt thanks.

Trademarks

All terms mentioned in this book that are known to be or are suspected of being trademarks or service marks have been appropriately capitalized. Alpha Books and Penguin Group (USA) Inc. cannot attest to the accuracy of this information. Use of a term in this book should not be regarded as affecting the validity of any trademark or service mark.

Part 1

The Fast-Paced World of Tuners

They've been called "pocket rockets," "super skates," and a lot of other things, but regardless of what you call them, modified Sport Compact Cars (SCCs)—or "tuners"—are indeed fast, furious, and FUN!

Your ride is really an extension of who you are, what you like, and the impression you want the world to have of you. So it stands to reason that you want your ride to stand out—to be as much of an individual as you are, right? Well, we know where you're coming from and we hear you.

Everyone wants to be special, and as you'll soon learn, the whole concept of customizing isn't a new idea, but there are certainly a few new twists to it when it comes to tuners. So strap on your seatbelt and let's put the hammer down as we take off on what's going to be a fun trip!

In Tune with the Times

In This Chapter

- ◆ What SCCs are and how they came about
- ◆ Makers from all around the world
- ◆ Customizing to make your ride special

In case you haven't noticed, the United States has been invaded—by sporty, compact cars manufactured in other countries. They're everywhere, literally. Just take a look down your own block, and chances are pretty good that the majority of cars you'll see are foreign makes. Take a closer look, and you'll probably see a great number of these vehicles fall into the category of "sport compact car." So this invasion is here in full force, with no prospects of letting up!

The Sport Compact Car Phenomenon

The sport compact car phenomenon came about for a number of reasons. The high cost of gasoline during the gas crunch of the 1970s spurred American car buyers to look for smaller vehicles of foreign manufacture that got better gas mileage and were overall more economical to own and run than their large, heavy gas-guzzling American counterparts. Overseas manufacturers were fast to respond, and this opened the floodgates for imports. Poor quality control across the board for American makes contributed heavily to the growing popularity of the imports, which generally received high marks in all of the automotive magazines and publications for better attention to detail, better construction, and just better all-around cars, to be blunt. From that point, their popularity just continued to escalate, and the invasion continued to pick up momentum.

What Exactly Is a Sport Compact Car?

Loosely defined, a sport compact is a high-performance version of a compact car or a subcompact car, and sport compact cars are frequently called by their abbreviated initials, SCC. These cars are usually front-engined, front-wheel-drive cars driven by a naturally aspirated (not supercharged or turbo-charged) straight four-cylinder gasoline engine. Typical sport compacts include Honda Civics, Accords, and Integras; Mitsubishi Eclipses; Toyota Camrys and Corollas; and more recently some domestics, such as Chevrolet Cavaliers, Dodge Neons, and the Ford Focus.

True sports cars are designed with a performance-oriented philosophy, often compromising cargo space, seating, gas mileage, drivability, and reliability, whereas the design philosophy of sport compacts is in sharp contrast—even hatchbacks (known as *hot hatches*) are in the game. SCCs are usually designed with a practical design philosophy and profit in mind. This philosophy has led to several compromises when it comes to performance, such as front-wheel drive, conservative engine design, and platform sharing. The ECMs (electronic control modules) in these cars are also programmed for optimal gas mileage.

TUNER TALK

Hot hatches refer to European-made sport compact cars that have hatchbacks.

Performance-oriented sport compacts focus on improving handling and increasing engine efficiency, rather than increasing engine size or converting to rear-wheel drive. For example, the Celica GT-S and RSX Type-S are both sport compacts that produce 100hp (horse power) per liter of displacement and have handling superior to their stock trims. This added performance, however, comes at a price because these models are expensive compared to true sports cars offering similar performance.

Where Do SCCs Come From?

It's hard to say exactly where, how, and when the SCC phenomenon started, but it followed a natural order of events with the proliferation of imported cars coming to these shores from Japan, Germany, and Korea that people would start making modifications to them shortly after their arrival. In automotive history, it has always been a given that somebody would try to change and/or improve a car as soon as it rolled off the assembly line, so why should imports be any different?

Historically, significant evidence indicates that import drag racing first started in southern California in the mid-1960s with Volkswagen Beetles, including documentation of quarter-mile passes published in *Hot Rod Magazine* as early as August of 1965. In the gearhead world, usually modifications made for cars on the drag strip almost immediately found their way onto the street scene.

In the early 1990s, front-wheel drive vehicles, mostly Hondas, gained popularity in southern California. Huge drag racing events at Palmdale, California, packed in over 10,000 spectators per day. Racers such as Stephen Papadakis, Ed Bergenholtz, and Myles Bautista dominated the first import drag racing circuit IDRA (Battle of the Imports) in the mid-1990s. Show car clubs became a huge factor within the import scene: southern California had *Team Kosoku*, and northern California had *Z. Team Yossi*. Since the days of hot rods in the 1950s and 1960s, car modifying has been very popular among young people in the United States, especially in southern California.

TUNER TRIVIA

The Yugo automobile got its name from the fact that it was manufactured in Yugoslavia.

TUNER TRIVIA

The island of Puerto Rico also has a long history of pioneering import drag racing in the mid-1970s and 1980s, and drag racing is still a huge sport on the island.

Figure 1.1

The immense popularity of sport compact cars and tuners is no better illustrated than at the numerous car shows, both local and national, that are held all around the country.

(*Dave Reider photo*)

It is probably safe to say that the movement for SCC customizing really got underway in the early 1990s, when enthusiasts in southern California began to modify compact Japanese cars, following similar trends in Japan.

When and Why Did SCCs Become So Popular?

Like anything new in the automotive world, SCCs presented a new challenge. The traditional American formula for going faster has typically been to increase engine displacement; the equation being bigger engines produce more horsepower, and more horsepower means going faster.

However, due to their diminutive size, SCCs don't allow for putting mammoth V8s under their hoods, and the fact that they are (almost exclusively) front-wheel drive vehicles further makes such engine swaps impractical. So the challenge is to squeeze more horsepower out of the existing engine, and car people in general love a challenge.

The fact that SCCs are more affordable than full-size vehicles doesn't hurt to raise their popularity factor either, and the proliferation of movies, such as *The Fast and the Furious* series, endows them with a lot of screen sex appeal for youthful audiences. All of these factors, plus a "new-school" way of thinking among younger car buyers, contribute significantly to the popularity of sport compact cars, and this trend has every indication of continuing well into the foreseeable future.

The Case for Customizing

Thanks to mass production, automakers are able to produce thousands upon thousands of exact copies of the same make and model automobile in exactly the same color with the same equipment. In this stereotypical, carbon-copy world, therefore, it's really no wonder that many people want to make their rides as individual as they are. Our First Amendment right to freedom of speech extends to freedom of expression as well, and customizing your ride lets you exercise that freedom. Customizing makes your ride something special, something out of the ordinary and unlike all the other cookie-cutter copies of that make and model on the road.

TUNER TRIVIA

In 2002, 30 percent of the cars sold were SUVs.

It is no surprise that when imported vehicles started to arrive in significant numbers, people naturally started to customize them. Some people are driven to make changes to things, especially their vehicles. These people are never satisfied with the status quo.

They desire to make their rides something truly different that will stand out in a crowd. We strongly suspect that you are one of these individuals. After all, you bought this book, didn't you?

IN THE KNOW

The ability to communicate is what sets humans apart from all other living things on this planet. And our ability to communicate allows us to express ourselves. Customizing your ride is just another way of manifesting your freedom of expression, so enjoy it and exercise it. Make your ride a personal expression of yourself. We encourage you to go for it!

The Origins of Customizing

Nobody knows for sure how, when, or where customizing really got started. Some folks have postulated that when the second Model T Ford rolled off the assembly line, an identical clone of the first one and the thousands of others that came after it, the owner of this second model decided he wanted to do things to it that would make it special and set it apart from all the others. It's quite possible, however, that customizing got its start even before that. It's really not that hard to imagine some early Roman chariot owner wanting his ride to look different from his neighbor's, now is it?

A History of Tinkering and Improving

An undeniable human trait is the desire to tinker in an effort to improve, change, or alter things in some way to make them different or better. Without a doubt, this trait sparked the first customizers who decided the motor car was fair game for them to work on.

Adding custom items to cars quickly evolved into the practice of modifying portions of the vehicle itself. During the 1920s, several high-end automobile manufacturers, such as Duesenberg, definitely sparked this practice when they produced the bare-running chassis (frame, motor, transmission, wheels, and so on), but no body for the car. Wealthy clientele had custom-made bodies fabricated and mounted onto these chassis, resulting in luxurious, one-of-a-kind vehicles. This was the era of opulence, and those wealthy enough owned these custom-made vehicles.

Thanks to Prohibition (January 1920–April 1933), bootleggers modified their rum-running cars to go faster in an ongoing effort to outrun the revenuers, and this gave birth to the American hot rod. Over the next couple of decades, modifiers began to pay attention to the looks of the vehicle rather than just concentrating on speed and performance, and customizing gained a foothold.

After World War II ended and the United States emerged victorious, throughout the land a can-do attitude sparked the spirits of many young men who had served their country. Now it was peace time; back home with some money in their pockets, they resumed their interests in tinkering and improving their cars. While some enjoyed making their cars go faster, others wanted to make them look better. Although both trains of thought seemed to be approaching vehicle modification from different ends, the basic drive was the same: improve the vehicle and make it different from all the rest.

Early Pioneers

By the early 1950s, the number of custom cars had grown to the point that the two factions—those interested in looks and those interested in speed—diverged and went off in their own directions. The custom car culture was born and, as is often the case with many new trends, California was the real seat of all the action.

> **TUNER TRIVIA**
>
> George Barris, the King of Kustoms, produced hundreds of awe-inspiring customs for television and movies, including the original Batmobile and the Munster Coach, in addition to scores of customs for private clients. From his facilities in north Hollywood, Barris still produces customs for clients the world over.

Customizing became a true art form by the early 1960s, with such immortal talents as Ken Howard, better known as Von Dutch, the legendary pin striper; and Ed "Big Daddy" Roth shaking up the custom scene with wild new creations.

Manufacturers: The Main Players

Before you can start customizing, there has to be a vehicle to start with. So it stands to reason then that the automobile manufacturers are the essential providers of the raw material for customizers. But who are they, and where do they hail from?

Makers from Around the Globe?

Although it's true that Japanese cars are largely responsible for the SCC phenomenon, let's not forget that the Volkswagen Beetle was rolling on the roads of the United States long before any Japanese-made vehicle ever landed here. The French Renault

Dauphine was also an early import, along with various Fiat models from Italy; Volvos from Sweden; and Coopers, Austins, MGs, and other marques from England; as well as BMWs, SAABs, and of course, Mercedes-Benzs, for several decades before the "Asian Invasion" started, as it has been called.

IN THE KNOW

Probably the first Japanese-made vehicle that we can rightly call an SCC is the Datsun 240Z, followed by its successors in the Z series, now going by the brand name of Nissan.

Today, here in the United States, vehicles from all around the world are bought and sold because we are just about the world's largest consumers of everything, including cars. So it's really no surprise that virtually every imported compact and sub-compact car has become fair game for the customizer as well as plenty of "domestic iron," too. And as the world's economies continue to improve and more and more countries become industrialized, we'll see additional brands of vehicles imported here from countries that previously had none to offer.

What that means for us is that there will be more cars to choose from and, because of increased competition, these cars will offer better quality, more power, and more features to gain market share in what has become an increasingly dog-eat-dog marketplace.

On the Domestic Front

American auto makers, once content to produce big, heavy, gas-guzzling land yachts, got a real wake-up call during the 1970s when the gasoline crisis caused rationing and odd/even days at the gas pumps. All of a sudden the compact foreign cars that had gone largely unnoticed by a huge segment of the American car-buying public now started to look good with their gasoline-sipping engines compared to gas-gulping American iron. That, coupled with better quality control for the imports than domestic manufacturers were offering, caused a lot of people to roll out the welcome mat for these foreign vehicles. And the rest, as they say, is history.

So American manufacturers had to play catch-up, and in the meantime, the imports continued to gain ground steadily.

While it took America a while to gain back lost ground (and it's still an ongoing battle), we're now seeing Chevy Cobalts, Ford Fusions, new-generation Mustangs,

TUNER TRIVIA

Monsieur Bibendum or Mr. Bib—the inflated "Michelin Man"—was introduced as Michelin's mascot in 1898.

PT Cruisers, and several other American marques become the subject of customizers as they make a very respectable showing for themselves at shows and cruise nights around the country. And this just goes to prove that a talented customizer can start with just about any base vehicle and transform it into something really special, regardless of where it originated.

General Motors has responded to the challenge imposed by the imports with a new Ecotec four-cylinder engine, which is designed specifically to be tuned. The engine is now being offered in the Saturn ION Redline and the Chevy Cobalt. Ford now offers many bolt-on performance parts for the Ford Focus. And aftermarket manufacturers galore have jumped on the bandwagon with performance and appearance parts for a number of domestic models.

How Big Is the Market?

Sport compacts are one of the fastest-growing segments of the performance car market. Manufacturers including Honda, Toyota, Mazda, and Nissan have begun producing "pre-tuned" sport compacts, such as the Honda Civic Si, Toyota Corolla XRS, Mazdaspeed 3, and Nissan Sentra SE-R Spec V. These models are often rebadged versions of models previously created for other markets or simply a trim level that was not available in the United States.

Toyota has gone so far as to create an entire division dedicated to producing customizable sport compacts called Scion. They place special emphasis on providing aftermarket-style accessories, such as decals, exhaust tips, and superchargers.

Obviously, with all this attention, the market segment is huge. In fact, SEMA (the Specialty Equipment Market Association) has cited the SCC/Tuner market as the fastest-growing segment for aftermarket performance and appearance parts, with annual sales in the multi-billion-dollar category.

Aftermarket Parts and Accessories

With all of these sport compact cars on the road, the public has a seemingly unquenchable thirst for performance and appearance parts for customizing these vehicles, and the aftermarket manufacturers have responded with an amazing assortment of products for virtually every conceivable brand and model out there. And the supply and variety continues to grow exponentially as new cars appear on the scene. As with every supply and demand situation, the manufacturers will continue to come out with new parts to satisfy the whims and desires of the buying public, so the prospects look bright for both the consumers and aftermarket manufacturers, at least in the foreseeable future.

Who Sells and Installs This Stuff?

You can get parts and accessories to customize the appearance and improve the performance of your ride from a variety of sources. Large automotive chains, such as Pep Boys, R&S Straus, and AutoZone, have huge assortments of goodies for SCC and tuner enthusiasts. And mail-order houses, most of whom have online websites for ordering and/or will mail you a catalog upon request, will ship your parts directly to your door.

Local shops and performance boutiques not only sell the parts but offer installation services as well. Their services include installations for virtually everything they sell, from audio systems to exhaust upgrades to engine modifications to superchargers to custom interiors and just about everything in between.

Even your neighborhood garage may be a source for installing some of the items you purchase via mail-order if you don't think you're up to doing it yourself. Local body shops will frequently accommodate custom paint jobs and graphic application work as well.

But as you'll find out on the following pages, you can handle most of the modifications you want to make to your ride yourself and, for the most part, you won't need specialized tools.

In many cases, it's like what Thomas Edison, American inventor of the light bulb (and over 1,090 other things), said: "Success is 10 percent inspiration and 90 percent perspiration."

The Least You Need to Know

- ◆ Sport compact cars have a lot of appeal to youthful car buyers.
- ◆ Manufacturers of Japanese cars are largely responsible for launching the popularity of SCCs in the United States.
- ◆ Customizing probably predates the automobile and may have started with the very first wheeled vehicles.
- ◆ Customizing your ride is a valid form of expressing your own individuality.

2

Different Types and Body Styles

In This Chapter

- ◆ Different body styles
- ◆ No rules to follow
- ◆ Turning an SCC into a tuner
- ◆ Getting good ideas from others

In an effort to give the public what it wants, automakers around the globe produce a number of different models hoping to satiate everyone's taste. This gives us a lot of grist for the mill, as it were, when it comes to customizing. There's something out there for every taste, and you can turn it into your own personal vision and expression of what works for you. And that's a good thing, indeed.

What a Body

The sheet metal that makes up the body of a car is the "clay" from which you'll model your ideal ride. Whether it's a sporty coupe, a three- or four-door model, a hatchback, a squarish van-type body, or an ultra mini, all is fair game when it comes to customizing. There really are no rules about what you can or can't do—or what you can or can't do it to, for that matter!

Variety Is the Spice of Life

Manufacturers give us so many choices because of the diversity of tastes when it comes to cars. What you like may not appeal to the next person; likewise, what he or she thinks is cool may not work at all for you. That's okay. The world would be a boring place indeed if everyone liked the same thing. Fortunately, that's not the case.

Figure 2.1

The Scion has become a favorite of customizers. Because you can order this "factory tuner" with a number of options right from the factory, it hits the ground running.

(Dave Reider photo)

Like the actual car makes and models, we have differences in types of customizing, too. There are the radical customs—cars that are absolutely outrageous and way off the beaten path when it comes to "mainstream" models (if there even is such a thing!). Then there is the more conservative train of thought when it comes to customs— different, but not "over-the-top" by a long shot. And of course, we have the mild customs that have very little done to them—perhaps some custom paint; maybe some attention to the lights, wheels, and tires; but nothing much more than that. Again, that's all okay; what appeals to *you* is what really matters here. After all, it's *your* ride, right?

So what type of car appeals to you? A mid-sized compact, a super-mini, a domestic, or an import? What about the body style—two-door, three-door, four-door, hatchback, mini-van, convertible, PT cruiser?

Figure 2.2

Convertibles are perennial favorites for customizing, and this Volkswagen ragtop is no exception. No rules really apply when it comes to customizing.

(Dave Reider photo)

Does Anything Work for Everything?

Those who are new to customizing frequently ask whether or not anything can work for everything, and the answer is surprisingly simple: no. The whole point of customizing is to take a stock vehicle and alter it in such a way that it appeals to the individual's personal taste. The purpose of the exercise is to take something that starts out the same as thousands of other copies and turn it into something different, something unique, something individual. That's why there is no "universal" treatment that works for everything. And that's something to be thankful for.

The SCC-to-Tuner Transition

Up to this point we've talked almost exclusively about SCCs, and with good reason: they're the basic raw material that "tuners" evolve from.

What Makes a Tuner a Tuner?

What is a tuner? That's a good question, and here's the succinct answer to it. A tuner is a stock or factory-default automobile, usually (but not exclusively) a compact or subcompact, that has had *aftermarket* modifications made to it that enhance speed, power, style, or all three of these qualities.

TUNER TALK

Aftermarket parts and equipment are those sold to consumers after the vehicle has been manufactured. Aftermarket equipment and parts are sold through Internet websites, catalogs, dealers, independent garages, and parts houses independent of the vehicle manufacturers.

Pick and Choose

If you're not entirely sure what you want to do to your ride, but you definitely know you want to do something to it, you'd do well to look at what other people have done. Magazines dedicated to tuners are a great place to start, and going to local cruise nights and car shows can also give you lots of ideas. You may see some interesting treatments others have used on their cars that you'd like to put on yours.

You'll find that just about everyone who's done any customizing at all to their ride is more than willing to talk about it; most people are delighted to tell you in great detail what they've done, how hard or easy it was to do, and even talk about the costs involved and give you pointers. You'll be amazed at how much information you can get simply by asking, so don't be shy!

IN THE KNOW

When you go to a cruise night or a car show, take a digital camera and photograph rides that you find interesting. Most digital cameras also have the capability of recording a short sound byte to accompany the picture, sort of like an audio caption, and this is handy for noting your comments or pertinent information about the interesting feature(s) that attracted you. If your camera can't record sound, then carry a small notebook and a pen. A camcorder is also another terrific way to record sights and sounds when it comes to idea-collecting at shows and cruise nights.

As we stated earlier, there are no rules—no right or wrong things you can do—only the things that you like. So think of your car in its present form as an empty plate that you can fill with styling ideas as you cruise through the "buffet" of the customizing scene. Let's say you like the wheels on this ride; the brakes on another; the paint on yet another car; the body kit on some other vehicle; and the performance, interior, and sound system mods from other cars as well. Imagine what a killer ride yours would be if you incorporated all of these ideas into your car! Go ahead; do it! That's what it's all about, remember?

Show, Go, or Both

Just about the only things that will limit what you do to your ride are your bank account and your creativity with the mods. Some people spend huge amounts of money on body mods, paint, and bling; others invest their funds in making their tuners land rockets; and others want the best of both worlds.

Figure 2.3

Even the Mini Cooper finds its way into tuner car shows. This Mini has received the full treatment, including a healthy dose of performance mods.

(Dave Reider photo)

IN THE KNOW

As you peruse tuner magazines, either mark the pages with interesting rides on them or cut out the photo(s) of the cars or particular customizations that interest you. Get a file folder and put these magazines and/or photos in it for safe keeping along with notes on what you like about the treatment, the make/model of the part or accessory, and any other information or comments that may be helpful when you review it at a later date. Great styling ideas aren't always original ideas but often an amalgam of several blended ideas.

You'll have to find a happy medium that works for you—a balance of looks and performance that you'll be happy with. Once you have created your vision, you can put things into motion.

Bragging Rights

You can consider these last three paragraphs as a sort of "pep talk" because that's what we intend them to be.

As you undoubtedly have already discovered, there are the talkers and the doers. The talkers are those people who constantly tell you what they would (or are going to) do to their ride. They have these grandiose plans and, more often than not, they're "experts" on all things automotive, especially when it comes to tuners.

Then there are the doers—the ones who quietly work out what they want to do to their rides and put their plans into action. When it's all over and done, the doers have their rides finished and are out enjoying cruising and showing them, while the talkers are still running their mouths with nothing to show for it.

When it comes to bragging rights, the doers win hands down. Because, in the final analysis, if your ride isn't done, then you really have nothing to brag about, do you? But then you already know that, 'cause you're a doer.

The Least You Need to Know

- When it comes to tuners, the choice of make, model, and body style is all a matter of personal preference.

- There are no rules for customizing—whatever suits your personal taste is all that really matters.

- You can get great customizing ideas by looking at what others have done with their rides in magazines, at car shows, and cruise nights.

- Don't be afraid to ask other tuner owners questions; most will be more than happy to answer them and talk to you about their rides.

Part 2

Getting Started

It's time to take stock of what you've got and what you want it to be. It really doesn't matter if you have a coupe, sedan, hatchback, convertible, a van, or even an SUV—you can turn it into a rolling work of art— something that's going to turn heads wherever you drive it—if you really want.

So what are you going to do to make it ultra-cool? What are your options? Are you good with tools? Are you willing to do the work yourself or would you rather "orchestrate" the whole operation and let someone else play the wrench and torch symphonies?

And how far do you want to take it? Do you want to go to the absolute extreme and make it a fire-breather that can only safely—and legally—be driven at the track, or do you want a super-cool street cruiser? These are all questions that you'll have to ask yourself. We'll help you find the answers in this part.

Chapter 3

Assessing Your Current Ride

In This Chapter

- ◆ What you've got to start with
- ◆ Exploring your options
- ◆ Determining your priorities
- ◆ Defining "street legal"

This chapter is all about taking stock of your current ride because it will be the basis for all the customization work you'll be doing. Or will it? Perhaps you'll decide it's really *not* the ideal ride for you, and you may want to work on another car instead; certainly, that's something you need to get sorted out now before you actually start to work on the car. Few things are worse than getting immersed in a customizing job and realizing, after you've already committed a considerable amount of time and money, that you wish you hadn't started it to begin with. Hopefully, after reading through these pages you'll be able to make an intelligent decision that you're comfortable and confident with, so let's get started.

You've Got to Start Somewhere

Because your ride—just as it stands now—is the raw material from which your custom will evolve, let's take an honest and critical assessment of your car.

How do you feel in general about your car? Are you really into it, is it just "okay" in your estimation, or do you wish you had something different altogether? If you really already dig your car, then just about anything you do to it will make a good thing better. If you're generally pleased with it, then customizing it will probably make you like it a bit more. On the other hand, if you're not thrilled with your car to begin with, customizing it may not be a great idea. At least it's something you should give more thought to before you invest any money or start any work on it.

Generally speaking, anytime you're enthused about a project you're working on, it usually turns out well because of the positive energy you put into it. But if you're only going into a project half-heartedly, don't expect excellent results because you aren't giving it your best shot. For these reasons, you need to do some soul searching before making the commitment to customize a car that you're really not enthusiastic about to begin with.

Figure 3.1

Taking stock of your ride just as it sits now means, in many ways, exploring the possibilities and exercising your imagination to get a vision of what it might look like when it's finished.

(Dave Reider photo)

The Raw Material

Okay, so let's examine the exterior of the vehicle. Do you see any dents, dings, or rust spots? If you do, make a note of them because you'll have to deal with them during the customizing process. Also make a note of any issues you notice with the glass of the vehicle—any cracks in the windows, pebble chips in the windshield, broken or cracked head- or tail-light lenses. How about the grille and other trim items; is everything in order there, too?

Next inspect the area under the hood. Is the engine compartment a dirty, dingy mess? Do you see any rust? Are the cables and wiring neatly wrapped with cable ties? Is anything missing or do things need to be replaced? Take notes.

Now move to the interior of the car. What's the condition of the upholstery? Is the headliner in good shape? What about the door panels? How about the dash and the gauges? Don't forget the back seat and the rear deck area as well as the kick panels and the speakers.

With the vehicle assessment out of the way, now you're ready to make some choices as to how far you want to go with the customizing; what areas of the vehicle you'll be working on and which ones you'll leave basically untouched; and whether you want to go mild, wild, or someplace in between the two extremes.

TUNER TRIVIA

Crude petroleum sold for 5 cents a barrel (55 gallons) in 1901! Compare that with today's price per gallon for gasoline!

What Could Work with Your Ride?

Both your desires and what is practically possible will answer this question. Some things aren't feasible or practical. For example, you certainly wouldn't want to stuff a huge V-8 engine into a Mini Cooper; to do a mod like that just isn't feasible from a physical standpoint. But you can do plenty of other customizing treatments that are not only feasible but won't break the bank, either.

Exploring Your Options

Everyone has individual tastes, and this is particularly true when it comes to cars. That's why you see so many different makes and models in so many different body styles and colors; manufacturers constantly strive to provide what the public wants. This is really an uphill battle for them, however, because individual tastes are so diverse. It's like Ricky Nelson said in his song "Garden Party": "You can't please everyone, so you gotta please yourself." That's where customizing comes in.

Figure 3.2

You've got to establish the "look" you're going for with your ride, whether it's mild, wild, or something in between. Think of your car as a blank canvas upon which you can create a custom ride that pleases you.

(Dave Reider photo)

What's Your Idea of Cool?

What rings your particular bells? Without a doubt, you have your particular favorites when it comes to vehicle makes and models, but where does it go from there? Maybe you want a unique paint job, some really outrageous graphics, or some very cool body kit parts. How about those really bling wheels with super-stopper brakes showing through them? Or perchance, you'd like a posh, palatial interior with a killer sound system and video goodies, too? And what about a super-tuned engine under the hood with some nitrous for extra punch? Do you like all these things, just some of them, or do you want something entirely different? It's all up to you; you decide and define what is cool when it comes to you.

How Much Do You Want to Do?

In realistic terms, to do everything that is the idealization of what a "cool ride" means to you may not be practical or affordable, so establish how close to this ideal you want to come. More often than not, this is just a matter of compromising.

For example, you may think that a totally chromed and powder-coated undercarriage looks super cool (which it does), and you'd like to do that to your ride. However, you probably use your car to get to your job, and it's your main means of transportation that you depend on, regardless of the weather. It's highly likely that the show cars you've seen are transported in enclosed trailers to keep them looking pristine, and they certainly aren't driven on wet, muddy streets through snow and slush. So while you certainly can do some under-carriage detailing to make things

TUNER TRIVIA

The rear window washer-wiper usually (but not exclusively) found on hatchbacks is sometimes referred to as a bidet (bidae) in tuner circles, especially in Europe.

look really nice, going full-tilt just isn't practical for a daily driver, at least not if you want to keep it looking like a show car.

Figure 3.3

Regardless of the make, model, and body style of your ride, you can do lots of trick things to customize it. Your imagination is limited only by your funds and how far you're willing to take it.

(Dave Reider photo)

Another thing to consider is that, in practical terms, going to extremes in customizing costs a lot of money. So you'll have to establish how far you want to go and how deep your pockets are in customizing your ride. It all boils down to planning practical and affordable mods while still producing the look and results you want to achieve.

DIY (Do It Yourself) or Pay Someone Else

You don't work for free, right? Right. Neither does anyone else. So for every aspect of customizing your ride that you can't do yourself, you'll have to pay someone to do it (unless you have a bunch of friends who are willing to donate their time and effort, but don't count on that to any large degree). The cost of outside labor can be quite considerable, so consider this as well when deciding what you're going to do to your ride. The out-of-the-pocket economics are also a real motivating factor for doing as much of the work yourself as you possibly can.

For the most part, the average person can do the majority of customizing work with a decent complement of tools, a willingness to put in the time and effort required, and a real desire to do a good job. Only purchasing outside services when you absolutely can't take care of them yourself can save you a bundle of money.

IN THE KNOW

The labor cost for custom work varies greatly depending on the kind of work, the locale, how busy the vendor is, and how fast you want the work done. For example, a custom leather and suede upholstery job may cost $1,000 in Tijuana, but the same upholstery work may command $3,000 or more in the NY-NJ-CT tri-state area. Be sure to shop around, ask to see examples of work the shop did for other clients, and ask for references.

A Work in Progress

Without a doubt you've seen your friends use their rides before they were totally "finished," right? For most of us, it's a fact of life that we'll have to use our vehicles while we're still working on them, and that's not a bad thing. The important thing to remember is that you *will* need to use the vehicle while you're working on it, so try to schedule your modification work so that it won't incapacitate your ride when you need to use it. For example, if you're replacing the gauges, gather everything you need before you disassemble the dash. Plan to complete the project and put the dash back together in one session so the car is ready to use when you need it, rather than riding around town with wires hanging down and some or all of your instrumentation inoperative.

Looks, Speed, Performance, Comfort?

When customizing your ride, deciding what you want to do is much like making a selection from a menu in a Chinese restaurant: choose one from Column A, two from Column B, one from Column C, one from Column D, etc. While that analogy certainly sounds humorous at first blush, it is, in truth, fairly accurate. What you have to do, in effect, is select and give priorities to the looks, speed, performance, and comfort aspects of your particular customization. Let's clarify this for you by taking a look at each aspect individually.

Looks

Let's start with looks. The looks of the vehicle involve a number of factors, including the overall color, graphics, stance, wheels and tires, body kits, and other attributes that contribute to the appearance of the ride.

First, decide on the color of the finished vehicle, and then select graphic treatments. Next, decide on the stance—how low the car will be to the ground overall, whether it will be level or have the rear slightly elevated, and what other attributes you want, such as how wide the overall stance will be. Then choose the wheel and tire combination(s) that will work for you. Also decide what body or lip kits you want to add to finish off the look of the car.

Speed

Speed is the next item on the menu. Do you want to simply increase the horsepower output a little, go a bit more aggressive, or go all-out to make it a fire-breathing pavement burner? As with the other aspects of customizing, the heavier you go with speed improvements, the higher the price tag goes. But there's more to it than just making the ride go faster; increased speed puts increased demands on the handling and performance, which is the next menu item.

Performance

Increasing performance means modifying the suspension system to make the car handle better not only on curves but also when it's going in a straight line. And better performance also means better stopping power, so the brakes come into play here as well as the traction control components, such as sway bars, struts, and shocks.

Comfort

Comfort is the last selection on our customizing menu, and one to which you should give some serious thought. Generally speaking, as you increase the performance of the suspension, the driver/passenger comfort decreases, due to the fact that performance suspensions are stiffer and somewhat harsher than stock suspension systems, so the ride is harder and not as "cushy" as the stock vehicle. Of course you can compensate for this by changing the seats and/or upholstery options so that you can still have a comfortable ride with high-performance suspension. But consider other comfort factors as well, including your sound system—FM, satellite radio, CD, MP3, or all of them. And don't forget the video items—GPS systems, DVD players, even game consoles.

One Big Project

Although customizing your ride is one big project overall, as you can see, several smaller aspects comprise and contribute to the whole. For the sake of getting a project plan together, make decisions on each of these four categories—looks, speed, performance, and comfort—and put them on paper. You may make some minor changes in your selections along the way, but at least this will give you an overall plan.

Put a numeric value from one to four next to each category to give them a weight of importance, one being the least important and four being the most important. Here's an example to give you an idea:

Looks = 4

Speed = 1

Performance = 2

Comfort = 3

From this example we can tell that this person wants his ride to look super cool with only a mild increase in horsepower, a little more attention to the performance aspects, and quite a bit of attention to the comfort aspects. Literally translated, this would sound something like a very *trick* paint job with graphics, bling wheels and tires, a minimal amount of engine work but a lot of clean-up and detailing under the hood, better shocks and brakes and a lot of attention to the seats, sound system, gauges, and other interior comfort items. Use this example to help you map out what your finished ideal ride will be, reflecting your tastes and values of importance.

> **TUNER TALK**
>
> **Trick** refers to anything that is custom, nonstandard, or otherwise out of the ordinary on a vehicle, such as a "trick" paint job. When a ride has a lot of trick stuff going on, it is said to be really "tricked out."

Setting Priorities

The whole purpose of deciding what you want to do to your ride is to set priorities for the order of the work. Obviously, the most important areas will require the most attention, which translates into the biggest expenditure of time and effort. Here's where that "weighting" system comes into play. For example, a category that you gave a weight of "4" to will take approximately four times as much time as a category you weighted as a "1." This isn't a hard and fast rule, but it does help give you an overall assessment of how long the project will take. Now, assign a time variable to each of these weights according to your schedule and how much time you can devote to working on the project.

Arbitrarily, let's say the time variable will be in weeks (although it could very well be months). Using this variable and the example cited earlier, the work on the "looks" of the car would take a total of four weeks, while the engine work and detailing would take only one week; the brakes and suspension work would take a couple of weeks, and the comfort (interior) work would take three weeks. Using this scale, you could finish the whole car in as little as eight weeks or a couple of months. In truth, this isn't realistic unless you can work on the ride full-time, but it serves well to give you an idea of how a project breaks down with regard to time requirements.

Setting priorities is important for getting the overall project completed, but you don't have to follow a given order for doing the work. While the exterior looks has a weight of "4," that doesn't mean that it's the first aspect that you would (or should) work on. You may elect to do the speed work and engine detailing first, perhaps next move onto the performance aspect with the brakes and suspension work, then work on the interior comfort, and do the exterior mods and paint last. The order is up to you and your budget, but setting the priorities is important, so do this now before actually beginning any work on the car. Get yourself a piece of paper and a pen, make your decisions as to what you want to do with your ride, assign these aspects weights, and chart out your priorities.

It's the Law

Unless you're going to be trailering your ride to various car shows, cruise nights, and other events and not driving it on the street, you must make it *street legal* to avoid problems with the local constabulary. So how do you know exactly what street legal is in your particular neck of the woods? That's easy to find out. Simply contact your state's division of motor vehicles and request information on the subject or go to any of your state's motor vehicle inspection facilities and make your inquiries.

TUNER TALK

According to *Wikipedia*, the free online encyclopedia, **street legal** refers to a vehicle such as an automobile, motorcycle, or light truck that is equipped and licensed for use on public roads. This will require specific configurations of lighting, signal lights, and safety equipment that need not be included in a vehicle used only off-road (such as a sandrail) that is trailered to its off-road operating area.

Generally speaking, being street legal requires (but is not limited to):

♦ Two outside mirrors if there is no line of vision out of the rear window

♦ Functional signal lights and corner reflectors

♦ Unobstructed view forward

- ◆ No frame modification (if built from another car)

- ◆ Front and rear seatbelts (for vehicles made in 1970 or later)

But there's more to being street legal than just adhering to these requirements, and compliance can and does vary from state to state, so be on the safe side and find out what's street legal in your state.

Flirting with Danger

Some modifications may or may not be legal, and if you're pulled over for a traffic violation, getting a citation may be at the discretion of the police officer. Things that may throw up a red flag to the police are:

- ◆ DVD or game console displays in the front passenger compartment (these can be construed as a distraction to the driver, especially if they are turned on when you get pulled over).

- ◆ Illuminated under-carriage neon or other lighting (especially if it is red, green, or amber, colors not legal to use on moving vehicles on public streets).

- ◆ Flashing or strobing lights—these may cause distractions to drivers of other vehicles on the road or be misinterpreted as emergency vehicle lights.

- ◆ Other devices or modifications that may be construed as being a distraction to other drivers.

Asking for Trouble

One of the reasons for modifying your ride is to make it stand out from the rest of the cars on the road, and you've customized it specifically to attract attention. But there is good attention and bad attention, and the latter is the kind you don't want to attract.

The police are always on the lookout for cars and drivers that may pose a safety threat to others on the road, and certain things are sure to attract the bad attention you really don't want to get. Avoid these things that are sure to get the police on your case:

- ◆ Driving like a jerk. Never be guilty of aggressive driving, such as darting in and out of lanes, passing on the shoulder, and otherwise posing a hazard to other cars on the road.

◆ Excessively loud stereo. Sure, the sound and the beat are cool to you, and you've spent a lot of money to make it loud, but all you're doing is attracting attention and asking for trouble by imposing your sounds on the rest of the world, particularly in slow-moving traffic.

◆ Burnouts and street racing. Leaving a patch of rubber as you pull away from a stop light may impress your friends, but it will be all but impossible to talk your way out of a ticket with such childish displays of immature behavior behind the wheel. And street racing is a definite no-no that will bring the man down on you hard and may even cost you your license.

Lastly, and we shouldn't even have to mention this, but drinking or taking drugs while driving is something no responsible driver does, and you are a responsible driver, aren't you?

Your cool-looking ride is the result of a lot of hard work and hard-earned dollars. Do not jeopardize it, your life, and the lives of others by acting like a jerk behind the wheel. Besides, if you cruise slowly, you give other folks a chance to eyeball your ride really well. And isn't that what it's really all about?

The Least You Need to Know

◆ An honest assessment of your current ride is essential before you start to do any physical work on it.

◆ You can do as much or as little as you want to make your ride the ideal example of what you personally want it to be.

◆ Everyone has different tastes in what looks good to them, so decide what's going to work for you.

◆ Making sure your ride conforms to all the legal requirements and driving responsibly are the best and safest ways to avoid hassles with the police.

4

Budgeting Time and Money

In This Chapter

◆ Creating a schedule and a budget

◆ Shopping for prices

◆ Getting the best deals

Time and money are both valuable—and finite—commodities. No one has either or both of them in unlimited quantities, so spending each one wisely is sage advice. It's amazing how both are intertwined and how wasting either one usually results in wasting the other. This chapter will give you information to help you use time and money to your best advantage and avoid wasting either of them.

There's Never Enough of Either

It's true that there's never enough time or money, and you can bank on that! Also there's a lot of truth to the expression "time is money" because one often equates with or has a significant bearing on the other. In fact, Queen Elizabeth I of England (who died in 1603) said on her deathbed, "All my possessions for a moment of time." While this is a bit dramatic, hopefully it will serve to drive home the point that time is, indeed, valuable and something that will come into play while planning and doing the actual customizing work on your ride.

What's Your Schedule Like?

Everybody's busy. That's why budgeting both your time and money is so important. Customizing your ride is definitely going to take time—either yours or whomever you enlist to do the work. If you're going to do all or most of the work yourself, then your time becomes very important; if you're going to have someone else do the work, then you'll pay for their time, so budgeting your money is important. And you'll also have to purchase parts and other items, perhaps some tools, so you can see that having a budget is essential to successfully completing the project. Let's look at the time element first, then the money element, and see how both figure into the equation.

Time for Work, Time for Play

While working on your ride may indeed be a recreational activity, it is definitely not play and you shouldn't consider it as such. Customizing your car is definitely work which will take time.

The first thing to do is decide how much time you're willing and able to devote to working on your ride. This is very important, so be honest with yourself. Are you willing to put in time in the evenings after you get home from work? If so, how many hours and how many evenings a week will you reserve for working on your car? How about weekends? Are you willing to work on Saturday or Sunday or both? Again, if you are willing, how many hours can you give on each of these days?

Now, remember that we said you have to decide how much time you're willing and *able* to devote. You may be *willing* to devote a lot more time than you're actually *able* to give. Remember to take into account family or relationship obligations, extracurricular activities, chores, and other responsibilities that are part of your regular schedule.

Also remember that all work and no play makes Jack (or Jill, for that matter) a dull person. Are you willing to give up social time with your friends to work on your ride? Be sure to leave enough time in your schedule to kick back and enjoy yourself with activities other than working in the garage. You certainly don't want to spend so much time working on the car that you begin to resent it. And that can happen if you don't leave enough time in your schedule for rest and relaxation. Remember, customizing your ride should be fun, not drudgery. Everything in moderation is the key.

Shopping for Prices

Now let's address the money end of budgeting. In order to create a realistic budget, you need an idea of what the entire cost of customizing your ride will be right from the outset. To do this, shop for prices and keep track of them either with a pen and paper or on your computer, whichever method is easier for you. Using spreadsheet software on a computer makes adjusting and recalculating the budget easier, but you can certainly do it longhand if you're more comfortable with that method.

Figure 4.1

Be sure to shop around for the best prices from multiple sources. The xenon headlight bulbs shown here were priced at $5.00 less than at the local auto parts store.

(Dave Reider photo)

Costs consist of prices for parts, supplies, gear, labor, and miscellaneous. This breakdown shows what each category encompasses:

- **Parts**—These are the actual components you add or use for the modifications, such as gauges, wheels, tires, and so on.

- **Supplies**—These are consumable items needed for various facets of the customizing, such as body filler, sandpaper, and hand cleaner.

- **Gear**—You may have to purchase tools or other equipment necessary for the project, such as an air chisel, a glue gun, or a steering wheel puller.

- **Labor**—This is the cost associated with any work or service used from an outside source, such as the labor for painting, engine building, or wheel balancing.

- **Miscellaneous**—This catch-all category covers just about anything that doesn't fit in any of the other categories, such as cable ties; gas and tolls to pick up parts; and books, CDs, or other reference materials.

Once you outline these categories in your budget planner, gather prices. It's important to keep records of what the part or service is, the part number if applicable, the vendor, the price of the item, and any associated cost such as shipping. Get prices from several different vendors or suppliers and compare them to get the best deal. For purposes of creating a cost budget, however, use the highest price; that way you'll be figuring on the high side rather than underestimating the costs.

IN THE KNOW

Part numbers are important since they pertain to a specific part for a specific make and model of vehicle. Using an air filter for a Chevrolet as an example, the particular air filter for a six-cylinder engine will have a different part number than the filter for a V8. So while they are both air filters for Chevy engines, they are for different models and they have different part numbers.

In addition to filling in the dollar costs on your budget sheets, also include a column for the time required for each aspect. It doesn't matter if you perform the work yourself or farm it out. If it takes time to do it, put the required time on the budget sheet. This will give you a more accurate idea of both the time and money you'll need to finish customizing your ride.

Here's an example of a budget sheet. For illustration purposes, we'll use "brakes" as our category.

Project Segment: Brakes—Total Funds Allocation: $300.00

Part	Part #	Supplier	Install Time	Cost
4 rotors	L27432	Abe's Brakes	2 hours (4 wheels)	$160
Front pads	L27432-F	Abe's Brakes	15 min./wheel	$40
Rear pads	L27432-R	Abe's Brakes	15 min./wheel	$40
Totals:			3 hours	$240

So from this example you can see that the work should take about 3 hours to complete, and the total cost for the parts is $240, or $60 less than what it was budgeted for. The exact numbers for the parts needed are also right here, as well as who the parts source is and a description of the part. Having it all written down like this eliminates a lot of unnecessary effort and confusion because it gives you a clear picture of what you need, where to get it, how much it will cost, and how long the job(s) should take to complete.

Discount Parts Clubs

Some of the bigger parts supply houses and catalog mail order vendors have parts clubs that may save you some money if you are a member of the club. Typically these clubs will give you 10-20 percent off your parts purchases once you exceed a certain threshold. This threshold can be $500, $1,000, or maybe $2,500; it varies from club to club and can also depend on the particular parts in question. For example, one club may give you a 10 percent discount on any complete exhaust system but a 20 percent discount on any wheel/tire package.

IN THE KNOW

If you know the exact part or parts you need and you've already shopped around for the best price, look for the same item(s) on eBay or other online auctions to see if you can get a better deal. But don't forget to add the shipping and handling charges onto the auction price of the item(s) to get a realistic amount of the final cost.

Like just about anything else, these parts clubs can have their good and bad sides, so don't be afraid to investigate them thoroughly. The good news is that you can save a substantial amount of money on certain purchases after you've satisfied the threshold requirement. The bad news is that you may be able to get some parts significantly cheaper from other suppliers, so shop around.

Getting the Best Deals

Don't be afraid to ask for discounts on your parts purchases right up front; some "horse trading" can go a long way. Speak with the vendor candidly, and explain what you intend to do with the ride from start to finish. More often than not, if the vendor is a good business person, it will benefit him to give you a package deal on everything you need at a discounted price to secure all of your business. Although this strategy will also work with mail-order parts suppliers, to negotiate on a one-to-one basis in person with a local supplier is usually easier. Some suppliers throw in free shipping with a large purchase, so don't be shy about asking if they'll include the shipping at no charge.

You can extend this strategy to labor as well. For example, the body shop you're thinking of using for the paint and graphics work may be willing to cut you a better deal if you enlist it to do the window tinting and some other work in addition to the paint. You'd be surprised at what you can get just by asking nicely.

Skill and Elbow Grease

One of the biggest ways to save money when customizing your ride is to do as much of the work yourself as possible. While not everyone possesses exceptional mechanical aptitude or tremendous skill with their hands, with some diligence, care, patience, and determination much of the work can be accomplished by the average person. And if you're particularly motivated to save money, that may be the added incentive you need to get you to roll up your own sleeves and dive right into it.

Are You a Wrench?

What exactly is a "wrench," you ask? Well, that's a moniker for a person who can use tools and, more importantly, isn't afraid to use them and get his or her hands dirty when necessary. Like all other practical skills, you become a "wrench" by actually working on cars; there's no substitute for hands-on experience. Although you can read all about how to do modifications and customizing in books, the real nitty-gritty of it all is in the actual doing of it.

So how do you know if you're a wrench or not? Well, ask yourself a few questions. For instance, have you ever changed your own flat tire? Have you ever changed the oil in your vehicle? How about changing the spark plugs and doing a tune-up? Have you replaced a muffler or changed an exhaust system? What about body work—have you worked with fiberglass, used bondo or other body fillers? Have you ever used a compressor and spray gun to paint a panel or an entire car?

Depending on how many times you answered "yes" to these questions, you're a wrench to some degree. If you answered yes only a few times, then you're a novice or, shall we say, a wrench in training. If you answered yes to all but a few, then you're already pretty experienced and savvy. Either way, you're probably up to doing a lot of the customizing we describe yourself. And that's a good thing.

Doing It Yourself

An incredible amount of satisfaction comes from working on your vehicle yourself. You'll gain a lot of insight about your ride, how it was actually put together, little things about the construction that you never knew, fascinating things about the engineering of the vehicle that you were totally unaware of. And you'll develop an intimacy with the vehicle that starts and continues to grow with doing hands-on things to it. You will not only get to know *about* your ride, but you'll also actually get to know *it*.

TUNER TRIVIA

Automotive pioneer Henry Ford sought ways to use agricultural products in industrial production, including soybean-based plastic for the body panels of automobiles including hoods, trunk lids, doors, and fenders.

Enlisting Outside Help

Without a doubt, you may want to enlist outside help for some aspects of customizing, whether it's because they require special equipment or skills you don't possess yourself. This outside help may come from friends, fellow tuner enthusiasts, or professional shops. Any of these sources are okay provided they know what they're doing and can get the job done.

You may want to consider a barter system for getting work done on your ride. The way this works is simple. You exchange your expertise and work on some area that you're good in on someone else's ride in exchange for his knowledge and effort to do something you need done. Let's say, for example, that you're a whiz at automotive electronics, but you're not too good at body work. You may strike a deal whereby you'll install a killer sound system in your buddy's car in exchange for his doing some body work on your ride. You both get what you need done and save some money on outside services at the same time.

Sweat Equity

You can also save money on outside services by electing to do a portion of the work yourself. For example, if you're going to have a body shop paint your ride, save a significant amount of cash by taking off a lot of parts that won't be painted and doing the *masking* yourself. Likewise, you can also cut down on the labor costs by doing the pre- and post-paint sanding yourself.

TUNER TALK

Masking refers to covering or shielding any parts or surfaces with tape, paper, sheet plastic, or another material to prevent paint overspray from getting on them. Masking tape and brown kraft masking paper are used by body shops for this purpose, and these materials are available at any well-stocked automotive supply store.

You may have some other skills or services to offer in exchange for work you need done on your ride, so don't be afraid to explore these possibilities with your prospective suppliers. It doesn't hurt to ask; you have a whole lot to gain and really nothing to lose by asking.

Plan for Success

It's hard to imagine any custom car coming together just by accident. If such a car exists, we've never seen it, that's for sure. On the contrary, every customized ride we've ever come across is the result of a lot of planning and hard work, with planning being the most important element. It all starts with a plan, and the best and most effective plans are the ones that are well thought out and logically put together. Ask just about any custom car builder you meet how it all started, and without reservation, most will tell you "it was all carefully planned" at the outset.

Don't underestimate the importance of a plan; it is literally the blueprint and roadmap for the work you'll be doing to your ride. Without a plan, you're like a boat adrift in the sea without a rudder: no direction, no destination, and no arrival time. A good plan will give you all of these; it's literally a project goal sheet that is broken down into incremental steps that progress from one phase to the next until everything is completed. When you complete the ride, the plan has served its purpose.

Stick with It

However, having a well laid-out plan will do you no good if you don't stick to it. As we stated earlier, the plan is your project goal sheet, so you must follow it in the order that you wrote it. Work on each increment as it appears in the plan.

In a well written plan, each increment is performed in an order that gets the car ready for the next increment. For example, when you remove parts from the engine and send them out for plating or other finishing work, engine clean-up and detailing should be the next step you perform, so that when the parts are finished, the engine is ready to receive them. Logical progression like this eliminates double-effort and needless work. Everything should flow together and proceed harmoniously. That's why it is absolutely imperative to stick with the plan once it is in place; skipping around is counter-productive, as it wastes time and produces confusion.

Here's a very abbreviated example of a plan to give you an idea of how to go about creating one for working on your ride:

PROJECT PLAN FOR ONE BAD STREET CRUISER

Project Start: January   **Project Completion:** April

January

Week 1

Go to Hot Import Nights show for ideas

Buy and read magazines for ideas

Talk to staff and customers at Import World store to get info on parts, costs, labor, etc.

Week 2

Prepare budget

Compile parts list

Surf Internet for best prices and sources

Decide what work will be farmed out

Week 3

Order parts

Check out potential vendors for farming out work

Prepare shop/work area

Check out tool inventory; buy anything needed

Week 4

Check and log parts in as deliveries arrive

Start installing body parts

List parts taken off for sale on eBay

Post "Parts for Sale" notices on local bulletin boards

Contract with outside service vendors

February

Week 5

Do bolt-on engine mods:

> Intake system

Ignition wires and plugs

Week 6

Install fuel rails

Install injectors

Install fuel pump

Week 7

Install coil-overs

Install front anti-sway bar

Install rear anti-sway bar

Week 8

Install big brake kit:

> Rotors

> Calipers

> Pads

> Stainless Brake Lines

March

Week 9

Install under-carriage neon

Install new dash gauges

Install new interior "mood" lights

Install GPS/DVD player

Carpentry—build sub-woofer box

Week 10

Finish sub-woofer box; check fit

Upholster sub-woofer box

Install speakers and route wiring

Install new carpeting

Week 11

Drop car off at Mike's Auto Body for paint

Remove trim parts and do masking

Take seats back home for reupholstering

Reupholster front buckets and back seat

Week 12

Bring seats back to Mike's Auto Body and install them

Help reinstalling trim taken off

Bring car back home and install new wheels

April 1

Take car to Cruise Night at Sal's Pizza

Watch them drool!

There are, of course, a lot of intermediate steps that go with each of these project goals, but this should certainly give you an idea of the basic framework for your project schedule.

YELLOW FLAG

Even though you have a plan and a schedule worked out, when you're not feeling well or when you have something on your mind that will distract you from giving it your full attention, it's better to give working on your ride a miss, because you won't do your best work. You can always make up for lost time in another work session by putting in some extra hours or working on a day that you ordinarily would have taken off.

And by all means, put commencement and completion dates on the plan, so that you have a timeline to follow. This will let you know at a glance if you're on, behind, or ahead of schedule. Keeping up with a schedule is as important as following the order to ensure that you complete your project correctly and on time.

Contingencies

There are bound to be some things that just won't come together according to your plan. This happens for a number of reasons, such as ordered parts not arriving when you expect them to or a personal issue preventing you from making the progress you had anticipated by this point in time. For this reason, it's good to have a contingency plan in place. If your schedule slips, it's not a big thing; it just means that you'll have to push everything ahead on the time schedule, so the anticipated completion date will be later than originally planned.

When these unforeseen things occur, you can usually move on ahead with something else on the plan that will need attention at some future time. This doesn't mean you should scrap the original plan and schedule; it just means you should substitute another item to make up for what you can't do now as originally scheduled. Sooner or later, you have to devote your attention to this aspect of the plan, so you can do it now rather than lose time on the project. You should always have a certain amount of flexibility in your plan to allow and compensate for unforeseen changes in the flow of progress.

TUNER TRIVIA

Several decades ago when Japanese-made motorcycles first appeared on the American scene, they were given the derogative name of "rice burners" by riders of American- and British-made motorcycles. This pejorative epithet then gradually started being used to cover Asian-made automobiles as well, although with heightened awareness of what is and is not politically correct, use of this term has declined significantly in recent years.

Adjusting as Required

Unless one has a crystal ball and some extraordinary psychic powers, nobody can see the future. The important thing is to revise the plan when required and then stick to the adjusted schedule so all still comes together in a timely fashion.

There will also undoubtedly be times when you just don't feel like working on your ride. It happens to everyone, so don't feel too bad about it. And if you're really not into it, you're probably better off missing that day because you won't be as productive as you'd be on a day when you really feel like working on it.

But also realize that whatever you don't do today, you'll have to do tomorrow or the next day or whenever; eventually it will have to be done. So don't beat yourself up about it, but do exercise some personal discipline when it comes to sticking to your work schedule. And if you need a little more work incentive, just keep thinking about how righteous your ride will be when you finish it.

The Least You Need to Know

- Time and money are both valuable, finite commodities that you should not waste.
- Creating a schedule and a budget will help you finish your customizing project in a timely and affordable manner.
- Always shop around to get the best prices.
- eBay and other online auction sites can frequently be excellent sources for parts at huge savings.
- Doing most of the work yourself will save you lots of money.
- It's necessary to follow a solid project plan; just adjust it as required.

Chapter 5

Tools Are Cool

In This Chapter

- ◆ An essential working environment
- ◆ Determining the tools
- ◆ Basic tools
- ◆ More advanced tools
- ◆ Working safely and preventing accidents

Regardless of what kind of work you'll be doing to customize your ride, you're going to need tools and a comfortable and safe environment in which to use them. And while you won't have to spend a fortune on acquiring tools, you'll have to make a basic expenditure to get the essential implements you need. As with just about everything else, you get what you pay for, so it's always a good idea to go with a better grade of tool because better tools last longer, do the job better, and are generally safer to use. As you've no doubt surmised by now, this chapter is all about the wonderful world of tools and your working space.

Where It All Gets Done

Think of the garage you work in as your base of operations, your private place and your *sanctum sanctorum*. It's a special place where you apply your imagination and efforts to transform a mundane, everyday vehicle into something special—a thing of beauty to behold and a very unique ride. So with these thoughts in mind, you realize that your garage is an important place. The better your work space is, the easier it will be for you to do good work.

Plenty of Room to Move

Finding a good location that provides you with shelter and plenty of room to move around in is essential for working on your ride. Ideally, a garage either attached to or adjacent to your home is the best way to go from a convenience standpoint, but you might also rent a garage or use one with the permission of a friend or relative. Of course, if the garage belongs to someone else, you'll have to be respectful of their wishes and avoid inconveniencing them in any way. That may mean that you can't work on your ride as early or as late as you may want to, you may have to keep the noise down (sometimes hard to do when using power equipment, such as air tools), and you may have other restrictions that wouldn't otherwise be present if you were working in your own garage.

Renting a garage may not always be the best solution, either. For example, many of the self-storage facilities prohibit working on vehicles on their premises, so check into what's allowed and what isn't before renting a garage facility. Now, with these caveats being given, let's consider some of the things you will absolutely need in the garage you do your mods in.

IN THE KNOW

Security is another feature that you shouldn't overlook when selecting a place to work in. You have a considerable investment in your vehicle, parts, and tools, and the world is unfortunately full of nefarious individuals who would like nothing better than to relieve you of your valuable possessions. Make sure your garage has secure locks, and an alarm system is also highly desirable.

Electrical Power

First and foremost, you'll need electrical outlets capable of handling the demands you'll be putting on them. Equipment such as grinders, buffing wheels, drills, and other power tools draw a considerable amount of current, so the garage should have circuit breakers rated at 15 amps or better so you won't be overloading them. If you'll be using tools such as air compressors or MIG welding equipment that draw a lot of current, plug these items into outlets that have their own dedicated breakers to avoid overloads. A few heavy-duty extension cords will also come in handy for supplying power when you're not conveniently near a wall outlet.

Self-retracting extension cords are great because when you finish using them, they stow neatly out of the way with a single tug. A wind-up cord reel is a good investment for easily storing extension cords, too.

Figure 5.1

An electrical cord winder/ basket makes stowing extension cords and droplight cords easy. These winder/baskets are inexpensive and great time savers, too.

(Tom Benford photo)

Lighting

You'll certainly need a lot of light while working on your ride, so make sure the garage has plenty of it available. In addition to windows (if your garage has them), several overhead lights should augment the sunlight while working during daylight hours, and lighting will become an even bigger factor when working evenings and nights. Fluorescent fixtures give off a lot of light without using much electricity, and they don't throw off any heat, which makes them desirable. Incandescent (light bulb) light is also acceptable, but you need high-wattage bulbs and several overhead fixtures to give proper illumination.

In addition to the built-in garage lighting, you'll also want to have one or two drop lights. While LED (Light Emitting Diode) droplights are preferable over fluorescent, either type is much better than those with incandescent bulbs. And, like extension cords, droplights with self-retracting cords are easier and faster to store. A flashlight will also come in handy for throwing additional light where you need it.

Ventilation

Ventilation, whether provided by windows, doors, or an HVAC system, is another prerequisite. You need fresh, clean air to breathe, especially if you're using adhesives, solvents, paints, dyes, or other chemicals that give off fumes and odors.

A small window fan or a floor-mounted pedestal unit will serve nicely for moving the air around in the garage but will also raise dust. So keep this in mind before you turn the fan on high. But that's also an incentive to keep your workspace clean and dust free.

YELLOW FLAG

While you may have a TV set and a DVD player in your garage, don't watch something on the screen while you're working. Regardless of how good a wrench you may be, you simply can't devote your full attention to both the task at hand and what's on the screen, and dividing your attention is an invitation for an accident to happen. Save your recreational viewing for when you take a work break or when you're done for the day, not while you're working.

Heating and Cooling

It's no fun to work on your ride when it's sweltering hot, and it's also difficult if not impossible to work on it when you're freezing, so some means of regulating the garage temperature is most desirable.

Of course, the ideal solution is having built-in heating and cooling provided by an HVAC unit. But we don't always get to work in ideal situations, do we?

A window-mounted air conditioner will do the trick for cooling, and an electric heater or an electric oil-filled radiator will help to warm things up when it's chilly.

YELLOW FLAG

Kerosene and propane heaters can throw off more heat, but they bring with them potential fire hazards as well as the dangers of asphyxiation from carbon monoxide; for these reasons, they're not the best way to go.

Necessary Amenities

You'll be spending a considerable amount of time working in the garage, so make it as pleasant as possible with some creature comforts. You won't want to be without a stereo to play your favorite tunes on, and a clock is another item you'll want to have, so you can keep track of the time. A calendar isn't a bad idea, either.

A refrigerator is a welcome accoutrement, and a sink for washing your hands is another great convenience. A toilet is wonderful, and a chair or two is great for taking a load off your feet. A phone is a good thing to have, as is a PC. You'll find it handy for looking up things, such as part suppliers and part numbers, as well as for checking and sending e-mail. A printer is also handy for printing out hard copies of the stuff you find on the web.

And there's a plethora of small items you probably won't give much thought to until you need them. Things such as paper, pens, pencils, tape, scissors, a can/bottle opener, a ruler/tape measure, a straight edge, magnifying glass, and razor blades, will certainly come in handy. Also include a workbench or table in the garage.

Things That Make Work Easier

When you stop to think about them, tools are wonderful devices that give you a mechanical advantage and permit you to do things you could not do with your bare hands, no matter how strong you are. Tools endow you with the power to tighten, loosen, cut, trim, snip, turn, bore, smooth, bend, stretch, compress, twist, pull, push, lift, and more. That's quite a bill of goods, wouldn't you say? And the really nice thing is that you can use the same tool(s) over and over again for all sorts of different tasks. And that, friends, is why tools are cool!

TUNER TRIVIA

A "monkey wrench" is an adjustable wrench that is rarely used today. It was invented by Charles Moncky in the 1800s, but through generations of misspellings, it became "monkey" wrench.

Tasks Determine Tools

This section heading pretty much says it all: the task you have at hand determines what you need in the way of tools. For example, if you're doing electrical work, you'll need wire strippers, a crimping tool, electrical tape, and possibly a digital multimeter or a soldering iron. It's a safe bet you won't need a 5-lb. deadblow hammer or a MIG welder. On the other hand, if you're installing a turbo kit, you'll need a socket set, wrenches, and screwdrivers. So the particular project dictates the tools required to get it done.

Now, while it isn't necessary to be as well-equipped as a NASCAR pit crew, you're going to need some basic tools regardless of how involved you intend to get in customizing your ride. You may already have most or all of these tools, or you may have to purchase them.

> **IN THE KNOW**
>
> When it comes to buying tools, don't be "penny wise and dollar foolish." Buying cheap tools is false economy because cheap tools do not last; sooner rather than later, you'll have to replace them. And by all means, stick with name brands, such as Craftsman, Husky, and Stanley. These are quality tools that won't break the bank, and the manufacturers stand behind them with a 100 percent replacement guarantee. If the tool fails or breaks, they'll replace it for free with no hassles. Quality tools are safer to use, too, because they fit and work correctly.

"Must-Have" Tools

To do the mods contained in this book, you need to have these essential tools. Some of the mods require additional tools or equipment, which you'll find later under the "Great If You've Got 'em" heading, but this section outlines the opening lineup of needed tools.

Screwdrivers

You just can't do without an assortment of good screwdrivers with hardened tips and comfortable handles. A minimum of three flat-blade and three Phillips head screwdrivers is essential, but more of each type in various lengths is highly desirable. For the flat-blade screwdrivers, get one thin, one medium, and one wide blade for starters. For the Phillips heads, get a #1, a #2, and a #3 blade, and add additional screwdrivers as you progress in your mechanical exploits. And remember, quality tools stand the test of time.

Also get yourself a rechargeable pistol-grip electric screwdriver. It's a great timesaver, very inexpensive, and definitely a worthwhile investment you'll use very often.

Pliers

A good starting pliers assortment will include at least one pair each of straight slip-joint pliers, long needle-nosed pliers, offset slip-joint pliers (also called water pump pliers), and side cutters. You can also include a pair or two of surgical hemostats (vein clamps), a pair of long tweezers, and spring-loaded, plunger-activated mechanical "fingers." These last two items are useful for retrieving small items, such as nuts or washers, that are inadvertently dropped into inaccessible places, something that will inevitably happen.

Figure 5.2

Assorted pliers will definitely come in handy for numerous tasks. Save some money by purchasing a matched set that includes the varieties you'll use most often.

(Tom Benford photo)

Wrenches

A good set of combination wrenches is indispensable. These wrenches have a box on one end and are open on the other. The box end is great for breaking a nut loose or tightening it, while the open end is used for removing the nut completely once it is loose. Gear wrenches are also great time- and work-savers. These nifty tools have a ratchet built into the box end and are great for getting at nuts where a regular socket won't fit.

Figure 5.3

A good set of combination wrenches is indispensable, and these flex-head combination gear wrenches do additional duty with their socket-and-ratchet like box end.

(Tom Benford photo)

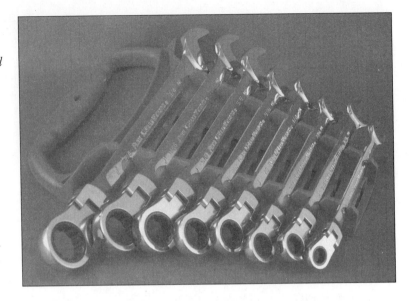

Also consider buying a set of line wrenches for work on your brake or fuel lines. These specially-reinforced box wrenches have openings cut into the boxes to allow the wrench to pass over the fuel or brake line to grasp the fitting. You can't use normal box wrenches for this work, and open-end wrenches are prone to rounding the edges of the fitting, so line wrenches are the way to go.

Hammers

Generally speaking, you'll need to use a hammer on very few occasions, but the need will arise at some point. A small brass mallet, a medium ballpeen hammer, a soft-faced rubber or rawhide mallet, and a 5-lb. sledge hammer will cover you pretty well here. (A claw hammer belongs with the household tools, not in your automotive tool chest.)

Sockets and Drivers

Your single largest outlay of cash for hand tools will be a good set of sockets and drivers. Sockets come in three sizes: ¼" drive, ⅜" drive, and ½" drive; they also come in shallow and deep lengths and in 6-point and 12-point versions. Get a couple extensions (6" and 12" should cover you here). While you'll use the ⅜" sockets most of the time, sometimes you'll need the ¼" set, and when doing heavy-duty work, the ½" set will be the way to go.

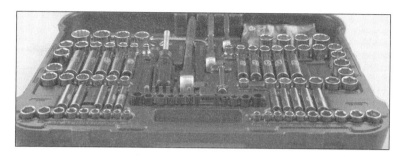

Figure 5.4

Save money by purchasing a socket set like this one from Craftsman Tools, available at any Sears store. The socket sizes are laser-etched so you can see them from a distance, and the set comes in a handy plastic storage case. Like all Craftsman tools, they are guaranteed for life.

(Tom Benford photo)

Hydraulic Floor Jack

A two-ton capacity jack is desirable, because it far exceeds the weight of any SCC ever made. With tools, invariably, stronger than necessary is definitely better. And by all means, stay away from the "bargain" import models; common sense tells you that a floor jack selling for $49.99 can't be anywhere near as good or as sturdy as one that sells for $199.95. Remember what I said earlier about false economy!

Figure 5.5

A good-quality hydraulic floor jack, or trolley jack as it is sometimes called, and sturdy jack stands are essential for safely lifting and supporting your ride while working on it.

(Tom Benford photo)

Jack Stands

Jack stands, which come in several varieties and a couple of sizes, support the car after you jack it up off the ground. Buy a pair (they're not sold individually) with a minimum of 2-ton capacity. The shorter ones are usually about 12" closed and 17" fully opened; the larger ones are usually 15" closed and 24" fully opened. The smaller ones are usually all you'll need, but get the larger ones if you're going to be doing major work under the car, such as changing the exhaust system or upgrading the rear suspension. Don't skimp here, either, because the jack stands will be the car's sole support while you're under it.

Torque Wrench

A good ½" torque wrench is all you really need, and you'll use it primarily for torqueing lug nuts to prevent warping the brake rotors or for advanced engine work. Torques come in three varieties: the old style that has a needle mounted near the handle, the newer style that clicks when you reach the desired torque setting, and the digital-readout torque wrench. Of the three, the clicking style is the most accurate.

Figure 5.6

A click-type torque wrench will serve you well if you're going to do any engine work that requires tightening bolts to a specific torque.

(*Tom Benford photo*)

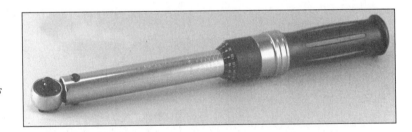

Lights

You must be able to see what you're working on, so good lighting is crucial. A small flashlight is a must, as is a good shop light. I prefer using a LED shop light with a 25' cord because it throws a lot of light and remains cool to the touch; it's also almost indestructible. The older drop lights with incandescent bulbs get much too hot, as do the quartz halogen shop lights. You can also buy shop lights that use fluorescent bulbs; these are inexpensive, remain cool, and throw lots of light but are fragile.

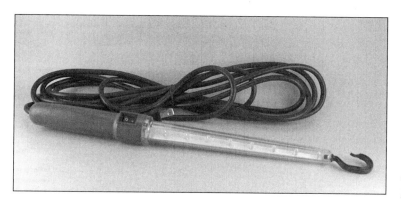

Figure 5.7

Portable shop lights are necessities. This light uses brilliant white LEDs to throw a huge amount of light, is virtually indestructible, and generates no heat. Fluorescent lights are inexpensive and don't give off any heat, but are on the fragile side, so avoid dropping or stepping on them. A pocket flashlight is another must-have.

(Tom Benford photo)

Electrical Tools

When doing any kind of automotive electrical work, a good digital multimeter is essential. Rather than just buying a general-purpose multimeter, however, go a few dollars more and get one that has automotive functions built in.

Figure 5.8

One of the most useful (and inexpensive) tools you can have for automotive electrical work is a circuit tester. To use it, attach the lead with the alligator clip to a known ground of the circuit you're testing, then touch the probe tip to a positive contact point. If the bulb inside the tester doesn't light up, there's a short or break somewhere in the circuit. It's also most useful for finding "hot" contacts.

(Tom Benford photo)

Also include a good pair of wire stripers and a crimping tool for crimping electrical connectors on wires as standard equipment in your electrical tool box. Electrical tape and a fuse puller are also must-haves, along with a utility knife and/or some single-edge razor blades. And don't forget to get a low-voltage circuit tester as well; it's a very useful tool for finding out what's hot and what's not in ride's circuitry.

Great if You Got 'em

These tools can definitely make your life easier when working on your ride and may be items you'll want to add to your tool arsenal.

Air Compressor

You don't have to get a large, industrial compressor that's the size of a refrigerator; one you can fill your tires with and power some air tools with is big enough. A compressor with a 30-gallon tank and 120PSI maximum pressure is more than adequate for any work you'll do.

Figure 5.9

Air compressors come in various sizes and in vertical (shown) or horizontal configurations. They are useful for powering air tools, inflating tires, and doing other tasks where pneumatic pressure is required. A good unit like this one costs about $350 or less at the local home center or automotive parts store.

(Tom Benford photo)

An automatic air hose reel is a worthwhile accessory item for the compressor. When you're done using the compressor, just give the hose a sharp tug, and it automatically reels back in. If you won't be using your compressor much, this is a luxury item; however, if you will be using the compressor often, you'll appreciate what a good investment an automatic reel can be.

Air Tools

Air tools use compressed air to gain a mechanical advantage and make jobs go faster. Don't spend a fortune on them; just get the tools you'll be using most of the time, and that includes a ⅜"-drive air ratchet and a ½"-drive impact wrench for heavy-duty jobs like working on suspension components. You may also want to add a set of metric impact sockets and a cut-off tool to your air tool arsenal for some of the projects in this book.

Digital Camera

What's a digital camera doing in the tool chapter, you ask? Trust us on this one, it belongs here. Taking things apart is usually a very straight-forward and easy process. Putting things back together, on the other hand, is usually tedious and often confusing. Here's where the digital camera comes in handy.

During disassembly, take some digital pictures so you'll have a reference for putting things back together. This can be especially important when you're interrupted in the middle of a project and your recollection of how things originally were is a bit fuzzy. The price on digital cameras has come down so much that you can get one that takes great pictures for less than the price of a quality socket set. It's also great for those before-and-after photos, as well as documenting your work.

Creeper

A mechanic's creeper is a nice item to have for doing under-car work, especially if you are working on tasks such as upgrading your exhaust system or installing undercarriage lighting. Because you can get a decent mechanic's creeper for well under $100, you may want to consider this piece of gear.

Figure 5.10

If you do a lot of work under your ride, then you'll find a padded mechanic's creeper like this one to be a worthwhile investment. The cushioning makes working on your back more comfortable, and the ball-bearing casters make rolling about on it easy.

(Mid America Motorworks photo)

IN THE KNOW

If you don't want to spend the money on a creeper, use a sheet of ¾"-thick Owens-Corning Energy Shield Outside Insulation. The stuff is light, cuts easily with a utility knife, and is very comfortable to use as a shield between you and the garage floor. Even cheaper is a large flattened corrugated box. While neither of these creeper alternatives are glamorous, they both do the trick and save you some bucks!

Work Bench

A work bench or work table is also a necessary piece of garage equipment. To save space, you may want to get a collapsible unit that folds compactly when not in use, although something stationary is more practical because you'll probably want to add a bench vise sooner or later. And it's also a good idea to have a stool or chair available so you can take a load off your feet when you want to take a break.

Renting and Borrowing Tools

Although you can expand your collection to include dial calipers, micrometers, specialized engine tools and sophisticated diagnostic equipment, you may rarely need to use these implements. If the occasion does arise, however, consider borrowing the tool from a friend or go to the local AutoZone where you can borrow the tool you need by leaving a refundable deposit. The local tool rental center is also another option.

Working Safely Is No Accident

Getting hurt or sustaining an injury is no fun, and if you're safety-minded, there really isn't any reason for injuries to happen. But creating a safe work environment and developing safe work habits doesn't happen all by itself. Indeed, working safely and creating a safe place to work is the result of deliberate planning, conscientious thought, and vigilance. Safety should always be first and foremost on your mind whenever you're working and with good reason: accidents happen when we least expect them.

Work Smart

Working on your ride should be an enjoyable pastime, and nothing will put a dampener on that enjoyment like getting hurt. While there's always a chance of injury anytime you're using tools or working with or on machinery, you can all but totally eliminate that chance by working smart.

Working smart simply means taking a careful and mature approach to the tasks at hand. Formulate a plan before you actually start to work. You don't have to chart this out on paper; just go over the particular project in your mind. Assess what you need to do; what tools, parts, or materials you need; and what steps are required to complete the project. By doing this, you'll have a clear idea of what's involved, and you'll be able to go about it in an orderly fashion, rather than jumping about willy-nilly. You will also find that taking this approach saves time and effort in addition to preventing injuries.

Prevention Versus Cure

The old adage "an ounce of prevention is worth a pound of cure," may sound trite, but it's true; it is much easier to prevent accidents than to cope with their consequences. Concentrate on what you're doing *before* and *while* you're doing it. Carelessness is by far the greatest source of injury in the garage and workshop, and you can easily prevent injuries by focusing your attention. Take a look around you for potential hazards—that air hose on the floor you can easily trip over, that tool on the fender that could fall off and hit you, that soldering iron on the work bench, that socket left on the floor, and so forth. Open your eyes, be aware of the potential hazards around you, and take the necessary measures to prevent accidents before they happen.

Good Work Habits

Developing good work habits goes a long way toward making your work in the garage safer as it increases your efficiency. Follow these tips for establishing good habits:

♦ When you're done using a tool, put it back where it belongs rather than leaving it on the floor or bench.

♦ Coil and stow that air hose out of harm's way.

♦ Use any solvents or other flammable liquids only with proper ventilation, and tightly cap and safely store them when not in use.

♦ Don't talk on the phone, joke with your friends, or watch TV while you're working. Dividing your attention with such distractions is asking for trouble.

♦ Don't work on your vehicle when you've been drinking; there's time enough for some cold beers when the job is done.

♦ Be especially careful when working with power tools; bad things can happen quickly.

Developing good work habits takes more effort than being a lazy wrench with sloppy work habits, but the extra effort pays off in the end with a safer working environment, fewer injuries, and less cleanup time at the end of the job.

Mandatory Safety Gear

You absolutely must have some items to work on your ride safely. These items include a good hydraulic floor jack (also called a trolley jack) to safely elevate your ride and a sturdy pair (or two) of jack stands to support while it's lifted.

Figure 5.11

Safety glasses come in many styles and colors so you can look good while protecting your eyes when working on your ride.

(Tom Benford photo)

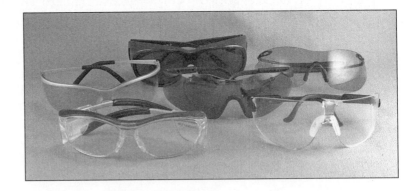

Always have a good pair of safety glasses to prevent eye injuries and a respirator to prevent dust particles and other harmful stuff from entering your lungs.

Figure 5.12

A respirator is excellent protection to keep dust and other harmful particles from entering your respiratory tract, especially when you are spraying or sanding.

(Tom Benford photo)

Protective clothing such as knee protectors, work shoes, and mechanics' gloves to prevent skinned knuckles are also on the list of required gear, as is an auto-dimming helmet if you're doing any MIG or TIG welding or plasma cutting.

Figure 5.13

Mechanics' gloves come in a variety of styles and offer excellent protection for your hands.

(Tom Benford photo)

Additional mandatory items for working safely include approved electrical extension cords, proper ventilation, adequate lighting, and protective footwear. We also highly recommend hearing protectors when you're using air tools.

First Aid

A decent first-aid kit is another necessary piece of gear. Regardless of how careful you may be, accidents *do* happen, and it pays to have a first-aid kit on hand to cope with such emergencies.

Figure 5.14

Have a well-stocked first-aid kit in every garage with bandages and other emergency essentials on hand in the event of an injury.

(Tom Benford photo)

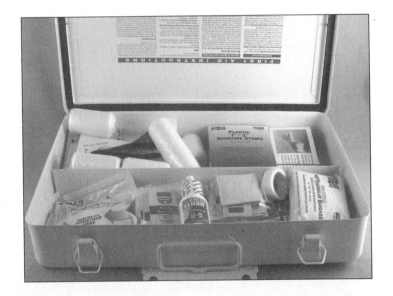

At the very minimum, have a bottle of peroxide and a box of band-aids on hand, but a first-aid kit with gauze bandages, antibiotic cream, and burn ointment along with other supplies is better. When it comes to first-aid, it's always better to have it on hand and not need it, than to need it and not have it available.

Fire Prevention

Nothing will ruin your day faster than a fire in the garage, and just about every fire is preventable. Don't leave oily rags, solvents, or other flammables lying around where they can pose a fire hazard. Don't smoke while working on your ride, and don't use any exposed flames around combustibles. Also be careful when using a grinder or stripping wheel, as the sparks thrown off can be enough to ignite a fire. And if you're using a drop light, don't use one that has a regular light bulb in it; a shattered bulb exposes the hot element for a second or two and that's enough to start a blaze. Fluorescent or LED work lights are better and safer.

Have at least one fully charged fire extinguisher on hand within easy reach. Fire extinguishers have different ratings according to the types of fires they can be used on. For example, Class A is for trash, wood, and paper fires; Class B is for liquids; and Class C is for electrical fires. Since you typically find all of these materials in a garage, a fire can involve some or all of them. For that reason, the ideal fire extinguisher for garage use is a general-purpose unit that can handle all three classes.

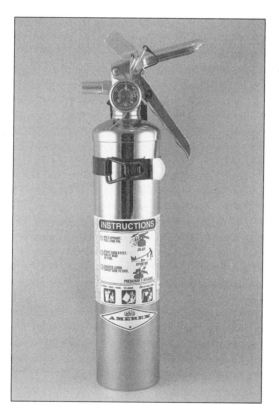

Figure 5.15

Have at least one all-purpose fire extinguisher available in your garage or workshop. Units like this one with a quick-release mounting bracket are the best.

(Tom Benford photo)

Most extinguishers come with a quick-release mounting bracket, just the ticket for use in the garage. Mount it where you can get to it in a hurry if the need arises, and don't pile stuff in front of it. Better yet, mount several extinguishers on all three walls. Again, better to be safe than sorry.

Remember, working safely on your ride is *no accident*—literally!

The Least You Need to Know

◆ A secure place with plenty of working room, adequate power, light, ventilation, and temperature control is a prerequisite for working on your ride. Developing good work habits will enable you to work more efficiently and safely.

◆ Kerosene and propane heaters can be fire hazards.

◆ The particular task determines which tool(s) you need for the job.

◆ Better tools cost a bit more but last longer and work better. Rent and borrow seldom-used tools rather than buying them.

◆ Air tools are great time and work savers.

◆ A decent first-aid kit and a fully-charged fire extinguisher are absolute necessities in your garage.

Part 3

Outward Appearances

Ever wonder why people refer to their rides as "she" or "her"? The answer is simple: a great-looking, sexy car is like a beautiful lady—a real treat for the eyes and something that gives you pleasure to look at no matter how many times you see it.

And because outward appearances are so important, that's where we're going to devote all of our attention now. Think of it as giving your ride a full makeover! We're going to go the full route here—everything from lights to grilles and hoods, to lip and body kits, mirrors, fenders, doors, deck lids, and more—literally, the whole nine yards!

And then, when we get everything just right, it's time to put on a sexy new "party dress"—some custom molding, killer paint, window tints, and in-your-face graphics should round it all out nicely! So what are you waiting for? Let's get started!

Chapter **6**

Front and Rear Lighting

In This Chapter

- Upgrading your bulbs
- Hi-intensity lighting
- Auxiliary lights
- Undercarriage and effects lighting
- Wiring and mounting your lights

Let there be lights! Yes, indeed—lights are good things to have on your ride, not only for appearance purposes but for safety's sake as well. So in case you haven't put two and two together yet, we're going to be focusing on lights in this chapter!

Burning Ever Brighter

Usually one of the first modifications is to upgrade a vehicle's stock lighting. There are several levels of lighting upgrades, starting with bulb replacement. Usually a twist-out, twist-in item, upgrade bulbs fit just as an OEM bulb would, although these aftermarket bulbs give you much brighter and whiter illumination. Many of today owner's manuals provide step-by-step instruction on how to replace the headlight bulbs, so that's a good place to start.

Better Bulbs

Some companies, such as Piaa, also feature a blue top coat that adds a light blue tint to headlights, and that augments the coolness factor. Other headlights, such as the ones made by Street Glow and Lite Glow, also offer lights with various power outputs and color tinting. It's a wise move to read the packages carefully because you don't want to use a bulb with excessive wattage; if you do, you may burn up your factory lighting harness, so be careful when doing this upgrade.

Figure 6.1

Aftermarket bulbs for upgrading your lighting are available in a variety of styles, intensities, and prices from several manufacturers. Most are simple twist-out, twist-in installations.

(Dave Reider photo)

Another popular bulb replacement option is switching to LED (light emitting diode) lighting, although this is more commonly used for tail lamps or brake lamps. LEDs produce significantly brighter light discharge than the stock units and last twice as long to boot.

In addition to upgraded replacement bulbs for headlights and taillights, several companies produce upgrade replacement bulbs for just about every bulb size out there including turn signals, parking lights, fog lights, and reverse lights.

HID Lighting

HID (high intensity discharge) lighting is like no other in that it affords you a much greater ability to see the roadway ahead of you than its halogen counterpart. Upgrading to a HID aftermarket system boosts your headlight illumination significantly. HID lighting also has an exceptionally long service life because the filaments do not fail due to everyday driving vibrations.

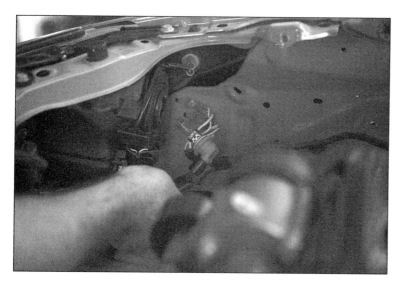

Figure 6.2

This HID bulb is plugged into the harness and ready to go into the headlight housing.

(Dave Reider photo)

When purchasing a HID kit, make sure you can get replacement parts for that kit. It is more likely that a ballast will go bad due to climate conditions than a bulb going out, but just to be on the safe side, make sure you can get replacement pieces if you need them. The last thing you want to do is to replace the entire kit because one component fails. A HID kit comes with the necessary ballasts (external transformers to generate the additional power needed for the bulbs), the special bulbs, and a pre-fab wiring harness.

Figure 6.3

When installing a HID ballast like the one shown here, note the plug-in positions for your factory wiring and the plug that goes out to the lights to make wiring simple. Don't forget to ground the unit as you see pointed out by the finger. The ballast is grounded to the inner fender in this installation.

(Dave Reider photo)

Installing a HID kit does require some electrical work under the hood of your car, but it's not difficult because it is predominantly a plug-and-play procedure. The ballasts are mounted under the hood, usually toward the front of the engine bay but away from the radiator. The car's factory wiring gets connected to the HID kits harness, which runs to the bulbs.

Although several of today's luxury cars, such as the Mercedes and Lexus, offer HID lighting as a factory option, companies such as Ignited Performance and Catz, among others, offer aftermarket kits for virtually every headlight bulb option.

Alternative Lenses

If you really want to go all-out when it comes to your lighting, you may opt to replace the factory headlight lenses with aftermarket projector lenses. Many brands are available with quite an array of combinations to choose from, including chrome to black to carbon fiber housings and single-, dual- or triple-projection with or without angle eyes. The options are quite extensive. Each lens kit includes the necessary wiring and bulbs.

Figure 6.4

This is a Subaru WRX with aftermarket headlight projector lenses installed. This common swap gives a cooler look and better illumination than the stock OEM lenses.

(Dave Reider photo)

And just as you can change your headlight lenses, you can give your taillights the custom lens treatment, too. Again you'll have a plethora of options with regard to the finish of the housing and standard halogen bulbs or LEDs, so there is something for everyone. Installation for both aftermarket headlight and taillight lenses usually requires some unbolting of the stock units and replacing them with the custom parts to the factory specs.

Figure 6.5

This Scion TC has the stock taillight lens.

(Dave Reider photo)

Figure 6.6

Here's the same Scion TC with an aftermarket LED lens. Quite a difference over the stock look, wouldn't you agree?

(Dave Reider photo)

Replacement housings for side marker lights, corner lights, and bumper lights are all available, too. It's a popular custom touch to replace the amber side marker or corner lights with clear lenses that have amber bulbs installed in them.

Auxiliary Lighting

Another popular custom modification that's quick and fairly easy to do is the addition of a set of fog lights. Though primarily thought of as a cool customizing addition, they are actually quite functional, especially if your vehicle didn't come with a factory-installed fog light option.

As with the majority of aftermarket parts and accessories, dozens of manufacturers are producing fog lamps in many shapes, sizes, and color options. But be careful here because sometimes these are not SAE- and DOT-compliant. Fog lights are usually installed on the lower valance of the front bumper, one on each side of the vehicle. But for those of you who are a little more daring, a stealth installation of fog lights can really give your ride a cool look. For example, mounting the lights behind a grill creates a really trick effect because you normally can't see the lights, but when they're on, the beams shine through your front grill.

The fog lamp kit includes the necessary mounting brackets and hardware for the installation. Also, provided instructions give you directions for the wiring, you can complete the mod in a couple of hours right in your driveway with basic tools.

Wiring and Mounting Supplemental Lighting

When installing supplemental lighting, such as fog lamps, running the wires properly usually takes more time than making the basic connections. What we're outlining here is generally true for the wiring of any additional lights, not just fog lamps.

The first electrical connection is the ground connection which provides the negative (ground) for the circuit. The ground lead is generally black in color and should be fastened to the frame or chassis of the vehicle close to the area where the lights are or will be mounted. The ground connection must be a good one, so use some sandpaper or a scraping tool to make sure the ground wire will be making contact with bare (not painted) metal.

Next, the constant power (positive) is run through a connection that goes directly to the battery. In virtually every kit, an in-line fuse is included somewhere on the constant power line. The fuse is a safety device that you should never bypass; it is there to take the brunt of any overload or short, and it's role is to pop, sacrificing itself to save the rest of the circuit (including your new lights).

IN THE KNOW

Clear silicone sealant (also called silicone caulking), available in tubes at any auto parts store or home center, serves nicely for sealing any holes you make in the firewall for wiring to pass through.

The last leg of the circuit is usually the on/off lead(s), which mount inside the vehicle and connect to a switch so you can turn the lights on and off. Always seal any holes in the firewall that you run any wires through to prevent water, moisture, and fumes from entering the cabin. Some kits include rubber grommets for this purpose, or you can purchase grommets at the local auto parts store.

It's also extremely important when running wires from the engine bay to avoid any moving engine components or excessively hot areas, such as around the exhaust manifold. Many companies provide pre-run harnesses with their kits that make it quite simple to run the wiring through your vehicle to the proper locations and connections; everything snaps into place, and they are even pre-wired to the included switch, so all you have to do is mount the switch with the supplied double-sided tape.

Undercarriage and Effects Lighting

Undercarriage lighting is a quick and easy way to set your ride apart from the rest of the crowd. Ready-to-install kits contain all you'll need and aren't hard to install. Under-car neon lighting is a great way to make yourself stand out at a local show or meet; having the whole floor around your car lit up and glowing will most definitely draw attention to you and your car.

Figure 6.7

A huge assortment of lighting effects products are available from several manufacturers such as these from Lite Glow Industries.

(Dave Reider photo)

Neon or LEDs

Companies, such as Street Glow and Light Glow, offer two- and four-tube neon under-car effect lighting kits that mount to the underside of your vehicle with supplied clips and screws. Strips of LED lights are also popular and are a bit more durable than their neon counterparts, albeit not as bright. The lighting bars (neon tubes or LED strips) are wired to each other to form a closed circuit and then to a transformer, which converts the power to 12 volts. Then, similar to the fog light mounting procedure we described earlier, you should make the ground connection to the chassis and connect the power line to a switch that you mount inside the vehicle.

Figure 6.8

This ride with really trick paint gets even more attention by using undercarriage LED lighting rather than neons. With this kind of lighting, you can see each individual LED rather than a continuous, glowing strip. Just more choices for you to make!

(Dave Reider photo)

Taboo Colors

If you are considering a neon or LED under-car lighting kit, we highly recommend that you avoid the colors that reflect emergency vehicle lighting, such as red, amber, and blue. Also be aware of your local laws because in many states under-car lighting is legal to own but illegal to have illuminated when the car is in motion. In simple terms, this means you cannot have them on when you are driving, but if you are relaxing in a parking lot with your friends or at a meet and the car is parked, you can show your colors legally. These color restrictions apply to the exterior of the vehicle; however, what you do inside your car is totally up to you. For interior neon and LEDs, the most common colors are blue and red, although you see purple and green used occasionally, too.

Strobes and Other Effects

Neon and LEDs are also often used as accent lighting in the interior and trunk of a vehicle. This popular type of lighting highlights trick accessories or installed electronics. For these installations, it is usually more desirable to install the lighting so that you don't see the actual bars or LEDs, but rather just the glow they produce.

Another popular addition is the use of strobe lights both for interior and exterior effects. Having strobes flash inside your vehicle when driving is a major no-no, but when you're at a show, strobe lights help direct attention to your vehicle.

Figure 6.9

This Subaru WRX has lights everywhere—undercarriage, trunk, and interior. Check out the trick lights in the door panels, too.

(Dave Reider photo)

Most people usually install strobes in their trunk or interior, although some builders have been known to install strobes in the engine bay as well. Installing strobes in the headlights and taillights of a vehicle is quite popular and can be a real attention grabber when you're at local events. Some companies make six- and eight-strobe kits meant specifically for headlight and taillight use that are close to actual police lights. Having them flash while driving is illegal and can get you a summons or your car impounded.

Mounting Locations

To install accessory lighting effects under the dash or beneath the front seats to bathe the floor in glowing color is common, and it's also quite popular to mount the bars behind equipment, such as amplifiers and speakers, to create a glow that highlights your modifications. Most times the light source is hidden from view, but in some instances, you may see the exposed neon tubes, especially when they are the effect style tubes, such as the crackling ones that jump to your music. Most times you see these tubes mounted near and around the audio equipment. They create a wild light show as your music plays.

Also sometimes people will install neon or LED lighting in the engine bay. However, this is most frequently done for show-only vehicles that usually see minimal to no actual driving time, because this accents the modifications done under the hood and serves no real practical purpose. When several under hood components are polished or chromed, the color effects produced by such lighting can be intriguing.

Electrical Work

You must be careful when installing neon in your project vehicle because these tubes are delicate, and if you drop or mishandle them, you may be out additional cash for replacement tubes. Both neon and LED lighting have standard installation methods such as those discussed earlier, and on most of these kits, the transformers are built in, eliminating an additional step for you.

TUNER TRIVIA

The winning average speed was 48 mph in the first Grand Prix race held in 1901!

As described earlier, look for a ground and power cable; the ground goes to bare chassis metal and the power lead is run to a switch for on/off control. A neat item available from virtually all of the neon manufacturers is a multi-box unit that permits connecting up to eight different tubes to one control box. This box lets you control the on/off functions and brightness. It even makes the light "dance" to the music through a microphone sensor built into the unit. Installing it consists of simply connecting all the tubes to the back of the box, then connecting the box to the power and ground. That's all it takes to have full custom lighting control at your fingertips.

The Least You Need to Know

- Changing bulbs is usually a simple twist-in/twist-out procedure.
- Neon and LED lighting can really make your car stand out at shows and meets.
- Certain neon colors are illegal for use while driving.
- Strobes installed in the headlights and taillights are illegal to have on while driving.
- Neon tubes are fragile, so handle them carefully during installation.

Chapter 7

Right Up Front

In This Chapter

- Factory grilles
- Aftermarket replacement grilles
- Replacement hoods
- Solid and see-thru hoods
- Hood fastening

You can do many mods to change the overall look of your ride, but perhaps none are so dramatic—or as easy to do—as those that alter the front, or face, of your car, the ones we cover in this chapter.

Prima Facie (On the Face of It)

The front of your car can rightly be called its face. And like human faces, it's the first thing most people see when they first lay eyes on your ride. Changing the grille and/or hood of the vehicle is a lot like performing plastic surgery on a human, only it's a lot easier and less expensive. And let's face it (pardon the pun); if you don't like the way it looks, you can always change it again!

Grilles

Changing the front grille of your vehicle can and will most definitely give your car a whole new appearance. Many of today's factory grilles are made of plastic and painted in either the color of the car or a black finish. Some car makes and models come with optional plastic chrome grilles, a nice bling touch right from the car manufacturer if you are lucky enough to get it!

Figure 7.1

Here's a really clean, sleek-looking mesh grille on a VW Jetta.

(Dave Reider photo)

However, replacing the plastic piece with a nice polished metal or chrome grille or perhaps a matte or textured black grille will really set your ride apart. And in many instances, if your car has an upper and lower grille, you can replace both to keep the new look for your vehicle consistent.

When shopping for a grille, know all of your vehicle's specific information, including the year, make, model, and sub model, too, as this information is necessary to make the correct purchase. Mass market grilles are prestamped from molds made to fit specific measurements. Or if you can be creative, go the extra mile and make your own grille. Either way the result will be a stand-out front end on your ride.

Figure 7.2

Check out the mouth on this Scion TC! Now that's what I call grille work!

(Dave Reider photo)

Aftermarket Grilles

Companies, such as Trendz and Grillcraft, offer direct replacement grilles for most of today's popular vehicles in an array of finishes and styles. Several companies even allow you to pick your grille's direction (vertical or horizontal) for models made of billet aluminum or steel. And all types of mesh are used to make grilles, too. Be sure to do your research because so many specialty companies are making grilles it's easy to get bewildered by all the options. And if you really want to be noticed, companies, such as DJ Motorsports, make grilles that include art, like flaming skulls and all kinds of wild patterns.

Installing an aftermarket grille is an easy way to make the front of your car stand out. Grille kits are specific-fit items that require the removal of the old grille and installation of the new grille—most of the time using the same mounting points as the one you just removed. In virtually any aftermarket grille package you purchase, detailed instructions will be provided. The average aftermarket grille installation won't take more than two hours in your driveway or garage, and usually you will need only the basic complement of automotive tools to do it.

IN THE KNOW

Sometimes changing the way your grille looks is only a spray can away. Often just spraying the grille with a contrasting color paint (e.g., white, flat black, silver, gold) can give the whole front of your ride a different look without spending more than a few dollars. For the best result, it's advisable to remove the grille from the car before spraying it.

Figure 7.3

This Chevy Trailblazer sure knows how to smile! Take a look at the four separate grille inserts that make up the front facia.

(Dave Reider photo)

Making Your Own

Assuming your desire to stand out is more pronounced, you can take things a step further by making your own grille inserts. Even with so many grille options available, sometimes you just want something totally unique that nobody else has, and that's when "rolling your own" is the ticket. Making your own grille is really a simple project if you have some patience and the right tools.

The first step in making your own grille is to decide what type of mesh you want to use; diamond, hexagon, oval, and woven wire are just a few examples of patterns you can choose. You can order mesh sheets online or, in many instances, your local Home Depot or Lowes may even stock your desired pattern(s). If your factory grille has a frame, use a hand-held die grinder, such as a Dremel, to cut out the center portions, and use the proper grinder attachments to smooth over all cut edges.

The next step is to lay that frame over the mesh material and use a marker or chalk to trace inside of the material. Using a pair of metal snips, cut the mesh along the outside of the marked line; never cut *on* the chalk line, so as to give yourself an extra ¼" for attachment. Depending on the mesh material you use, a two-step clear epoxy will usually do the trick for attachment. Follow the mixing directions that came with the epoxy exactly. Put a fine bead of epoxy along the rear edge of the grille frame and lay the mesh on top. Let it cure overnight, and that's all there is to making a custom grille. Install it back into the car using the same fasteners that held it originally, and you're done. That was easy enough, wasn't it?

Hoods

An aftermarket hood can be a nice complement to a custom grille or a body kit, and, in some cases, a builder will choose the hood before making any other modifications. Aftermarket hoods not only offer style, but they can also provide functional performance enhancements at the same time.

Metal, Glass, and Carbon Fiber Hoods

As with just about all other aftermarket parts, the available hoods give you a multitude of choices. Metal, fiberglass, Plexiglas, and carbon fiber are the materials of choice used, and the odds are excellent that you can find an aftermarket hood for your car that works for you.

Figure 7.4

Here's an example of a stock Scion TC hood.

(Dave Reider photo)

The first step is to decide what style or theme you want to use. Chances are pretty good that if you're building a performance machine, a heavy metal or see-thru Plexiglas hood isn't going to be a good choice for you because these are intended more for show than go. If, on the other hand, you're building an all-show motor with lots of chrome and polished parts, you'd do well to consider a Plexiglas hood to show off all that bling.

Form and Function

There are many styles of aftermarket hoods; some are meant strictly for looks, whereas others actually enhance the airflow over the vehicle. Also in some cases hood replacement becomes necessary because particular engine modifications rise above your standard factory hood's height. Whatever the reason, consider two important criteria when in the market for a new hood. Once you know what style you are looking for, the first option is the form. You'll have to decide about the hood's form itself. Do you want it raised or flat, vented or not vented, ram-air or cowl induction? This choice is all up to you, so go with your own personal preference. The second is function. If you're replacing your hood for better air flow, ram-air, or cowl induction styles to cool your engine better or for clearance purposes for a functional reason, explore all available aftermarket options to find the best hood for your needs and budget.

Figure 7.6

European cars always have a lot of style and class, and this example of a true DTM hood looks like it grew there.

(Dave Reider photo)

See-Thru Hoods

More common for show car competitors are clear or color-tinted Plexiglas hoods made by companies, such as Euro Hoods, which make quality see-thru hoods for most applications. This type of hood is primarily meant for show purposes and should not be used on a daily-driven car. Though an acrylic hood is reasonably durable, it is still susceptible to excessive heat warping and discoloration due to natural environmental conditions, in addition to pebble nicks and scratches. If you are really set on having a Plexiglas hood and your vehicle is driven daily, you might want to consider having a custom hood that you install for cruise nights and car shows and using the stock hood the rest of the time.

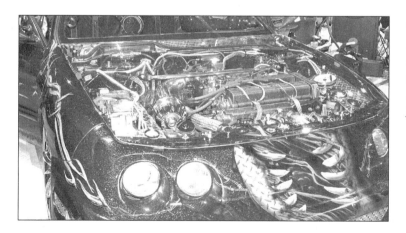

Figure 7.7

Here's a great example of a clear hood—great to show off all your engine details at shows but, alas, not practical for a daily driver!

(Dave Reider photo)

Ram-Air Hoods

Ram-air is as descriptive as names for hoods get. A ram-air hood has raised openings, and the motion of the car literally rams air through these vents forcing it into your engine bay. In many instances a ram-air hood will be connected via appropriate duct work to force this air directly into your vehicle's intake, thus increasing engine power output. In all honesty, with this modification, there probably is not enough of a performance gain for you to feel a difference, but you will notice that your car runs cooler than it used to. Even if you don't have a truly functional ram-air setup, this type of hood by itself will still force more natural air into the engine bay so the motor runs cooler; a cooler running engine is beneficial in any vehicle.

Figure 7.8

A very cool ram-air hood on this Subaru WRX looks good and is a functional performance mod as well.

(Dave Reider photo)

Cowl Induction Hoods

Similar in function to a ram-air hood, a cowl-induction hood sits a bit taller on the car. Usually this type of hood is used on vehicles where engine modifications necessitate using a higher-clearance hood. Cowl-induction hoods are made in a variety of rises from one inch all the way up to as high as four inches, so you'll likely find something to fit your needs. Another benefit of these hoods is that they are usually vented at the rear. When the airflow hits the hood, it travels up the cowl and hits the windshield; the deflected air then flows back into the vented cowl opening, directing fresh cool air onto the motor as well.

Hood Replacement

The first step is to unlatch your factory hood and prop it up with an assistant on each side supporting the hood. Use the proper socket and ratchet to remove the bolts (usually three) that connect the hood to the hinge on one side, and then repeat the process on the other side. As your assistants carefully lift the hood away from the car, place the bolts in a zip-lock bag for the time being and label that bag accordingly. Remove the bolts that secure the latching mechanism, and store them safely as well.

Confirm that the aftermarket hood has mounting holes to accommodate the latching mechanism. If it does, install the latching mechanism in the new hood using the same hardware you removed from the old unit.

However, on many aftermarket hoods the latching mechanisms are not accommodated, so you'll need to purchase a separate set of hood pins (installing them is covered later in this chapter).

YELLOW FLAG

Hood replacement is generally a simple operation, though it is a multi-person task; *never* try to perform this modification on your own. It's not that you can't do it alone, but don't risk damaging your vehicle (a high likelihood). It's best to have two assistants holding the old hood in place as you unbolt it and to align the new hood up as you bolt it back on.

Have your two assistants hold the hood over the engine and test the fit of the hood by making sure it sits between the fenders. Once this checks out, have the assistants hold the hood in the propped position so you can reinstall the bolts you removed earlier and secure the new hood on the factory hinges.

Now, with the bolts inserted properly, slowly and carefully lower your hood into the latching position, making sure the fit is correct. This may take several tries; adjust the hood each time by loosening up the bolts to give it a little shift and retightening. When the hood fit is correct, securely tighten the bolts.

IN THE KNOW

Remember to label the bolts as you remove them from the original hood; this is important because, even though they all came from the same hinge, there may be important differences between them that can affect their installation in the new hood if not correctly oriented.

Pinning It Down

As mentioned earlier, some aftermarket hoods don't accommodate factory hood latches; optionally, you elect to use a set of hood pins just because they are out right cool. Whatever the reason for using them, hood pins are a secondary safety measure for latching hoods and almost a necessity on any car going to the track.

Install hood pins on the front radiator support of your vehicle, and they protrude through holes in the hood that you must carefully and precisely drill (templates for drilling and mounting are usually supplied with the hood pin kit).

Figure 7.9

A typical hood pin kit is shown here. This is a virtual necessity with some aftermarket hoods, but it looks cool even when installed on a stock hood.

(Dave Reider photo)

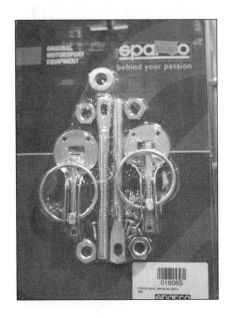

There are several different types and styles of hood pins, though the most common for tuners is the simple standard push-pin. Companies, such as Hoodpins.com, offer a higher end product that is self-latching; this type of product alleviates the worrying about remembering if you did or did not put the pins back in before you use the car. The last thing you want to experience is your hood flying up to where it meets the windshield while you're driving!

The Least You Need to Know

- ◆ Changing the grille(s) can dramatically alter the appearance of your car.

- ◆ Aftermarket grilles come in a variety of styles or you can make your own from readily-available mesh materials.

- ◆ Aftermarket hoods can be functional as well as eye-catching.

- ◆ See-through Plexiglas hoods are better suited to show-only vehicles than to daily drivers.

- ◆ Aftermarket hoods may require the use of hood pins to keep them closed.

Chapter 8

Body Parts

In This Chapter

- ◆ Body skirts
- ◆ Factory and aftermarket lip kits
- ◆ Mirrors and mountings
- ◆ Fenders, doors, and more

Adding extra lower moldings to the car body is an easy and relatively inexpensive way to dramatically alter the appearance of your ride, but that's not all you can do. Additionally, you can add custom touches like changing the mirrors, perhaps going with wide-body fenders, custom doors, and even more. As with most customizing choices, you have lots of options to explore in doing a body makeover, which is what we cover in this chapter.

Lip and Body Kits

To start off the body makeover, we start with the lips and kits.

Skirting the Issues

Adding additional panels or elongated panels to give the car body a lower appearance is known as *skirting* in some custom car circles.

TUNER TALK

Skirting refers to the installation of lip and/or body kits.

Figure 8.1

This is a fiberglass lip kit for a Scion XB in its raw state. You must prep and paint these parts before installing them.

(Andy Goodman photo)

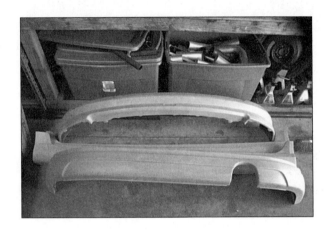

The Material Matters

As is usually the case when so many exterior options are available, deciding what route to go becomes quite difficult. Not only are there several different types of aftermarket body panels available, but to add to the confusion, there are also three common types of material to choose from: urethane, fiberglass, and carbon fiber. Let's take a minute or two and explain the differences.

Urethane is not as popular as the other materials used for these parts, but it's a good investment for longevity. Urethane is a good material choice; it's flexible, so it can take more abuse than the other materials. Because of this flexibility, if a urethane bumper or side skirt takes a hit, you can leave it in the sun, and the heat will cause it to mend back to its original shape on its own. That is, of course, provided that we're talking about a simple dent. You will still probably have to do some paint work to cover the ding, but it's still a lot better than having to replace the piece, as would be the case with fiberglass or carbon fiber.

Figure 8.2

Most people would believe that the lip on this Acura TSX came with the car because it looks so original. But they'd be wrong—it's an aftermarket product.

(Dave Reider photo)

Fiberglass is the next material choice, and it is a favorite over urethane because it weighs much less. The downside of fiberglass is that it is not as strong as urethane when taking a direct hit and is more susceptible to cracking. Fiberglass panels are more commonly used for hoods, since they are less likely to be subjected to direct impacts. Another benefit for fiberglass is that it can afford you a limitless amount of exterior customizing possibilities due to the fact that it is easy-to-mold. Fiberglass is also frequently used for doing headlight or taillight conversions because it is easily formed for custom shapes.

IN THE KNOW

Headlight or taillight conversions consist of taking a headlight or taillight from a certain make and model vehicle and fitting it into another, totally different car. More often than not, to do this effectively requires quite a large amount of body work and a bit of skill.

Carbon fiber is definitely the most-used material choice of modern tuners worldwide. Having the durability of urethane yet the weight of fiberglass, carbon fiber is truly the material of the future. In fact, it seems that just about everything aftermarket is being made in carbon fiber: bumpers, hoods, fenders, doors, trunk lids, and side mirrors; you name it and you can probably find it in carbon fiber. Carbon fiber is a woven material that, if used correctly, is stronger then metal. Many companies, such as Carbon Creation, specialize in carbon fiber components that are readily available.

Figure 8.3

Here's a stock Scion TC front bumper. Contrast this with the aftermarket front bumper on the TC.

(Dave Reider photo)

Figure 8.4

This is the trick aftermarket front bumper on this TC. Some difference, isn't there?

(Dave Reider photo)

Factory-Option Lip Kits

With today's popularity in automotive customizing, many auto manufacturers themselves are offering factory-option *lip kits*. This means you can order your car directly from the factory with an optional lip kit installed right on the assembly line.

TUNER TALK

Lip kit is a term used to describe aftermarket body enhancement panels that get mounted to the lower valance of the factory bumpers and lower sides between the front and rear wheel wells. Lip kits provide a sporty lower appearance while adding better aerodynamics to your vehicle.

Figure 8.5

Would you have guessed that this cool ride started out as stock Mazda RX7?

(Dave Reider photo)

A plus for ordering the factory option kit is the financing: add any factory offered item from the dealer to your financing charges at the dealership at the time of purchase and for a few extra dollars a month you have a sleeker, more stylish ride. However you decide to go, these kits are a terrific way to get started in the world of automotive accessorizing.

YELLOW FLAG

Many times these "factory option" kits, though labeled by the vehicle manufactures as their own, are really produced by one of the known aftermarket manufactures from within the industry. Although this is, in itself, not a bad thing, if you are on a tight budget, you may very well find the same product in an aftermarket shop at a much lower price. Bear in mind, however, you will need to install it yourself or have it installed and painted.

Aftermarket Kits

Your choices are much greater when it comes to selecting aftermarket kits to customize your ride. Dozens of companies produce aftermarket kits for all makes and models. With all the choices available, the question becomes one of quality versus cost. Of course, as with purchasing anything where you have multiple choices for the same item, the choice comes down to deciding whether to sacrifice quality to get what you want now or waiting and saving a while longer to get that exotic imported kit that will set your ride apart from the others.

Of course, trying to figure out what style kit is right for you can be another extremely difficult decision. Some enthusiasts want that really wild look that stands out, so they go for a flashy Showgun or Black Widow themed kit. Conversely, a performance-oriented builder would probably be eyeing a Du-Luck or Junction Products kit. Though obtainable (albeit with perhaps some difficulty), the hard-core enthusiast recognizes these types of kits as really top-drawer and they appeal to the elite tuner. Those who really go all out may make the extremely expensive investment and purchase what could rightly be the ultimate, never-could-be-duplicated Veilside Fortune kit.

Multi-Piece Body Kits with Bumpers

When you go shopping for a *body kit*, you'll hear terms such as four-, five- or even six-piece kits. Here's the component breakdown, short and simple: a 4-pc. kit consists of a front and rear bumper and a left and right side skirt. A 5-pc. kit would include the addition of a rear wing that mounts to the deck lid. Kicking it up a notch further, a 6-pc. kit adds a custom hood to the mix. And if that's still not enough for you, kits such as the Veilside Fortune Kits include replacement widened fenders, widened door skins, and widened quarter panels to give you the ever-so-desirable ultimate wide body vehicle. All of this is in addition to the bumpers, side skirts, and wings.

> **TUNER TALK**
>
> A **body kit** is a set of aftermarket components that are usually direct bolt-on replacements for factory parts and a body kit can include a hood or a hood scoop, a spoiler, a rear wing and other components, depending on the manufacturer, price and make and model on which it is intended to be used.

Figure 8.6

This Subaru WRX has the full body treatment—aftermarket front and rear bumpers, side skirts, custom mirrors, hood and rear deck wing—the whole nine yards!

(Dave Reider photo)

Bear in mind, however, no rule forces you to purchase a full kit from any one company. In many instances a builder can and will mix and match the components he likes. Say he chooses a front bumper from one company, a rear bumper from another, and the side skirts from yet a third, different company to create his own individual look and feel. This method is usually a bit more costly than purchasing the all-parts-included kit, but then again, it's individuality that makes this hobby great. And you are going for an individual look, aren't you?

Mirrors and More

Mirrors do a lot more than just let you see what's behind you. Indeed, they are integral to the overall look and theme of your ride. Making the rest of the car custom and leaving the mirrors stock can be a big mistake and something you definitely do not want to overlook.

Side-View Mirror Options

Now that you've spent all that time and energy deciding on what body kit or mix of various components you want to use, there's yet more decisions ahead. The one exterior component that does not come with your standard body kit is, you've probably guessed it by now, side-view mirrors. And just as you had dozens of body kit choices, you have all different styles of side-view mirrors to choose from as well. Big, small, with lights, without lights, with blinkers or not, the list just keeps going on and on. The most popular style would probably be the Euro-themed, or what we will call M3-style, mirrors, which have a sleek, streamlined appearance to them. Produced by a number of companies, these really stand out.

Figure 8.7

Notice this very cool set of aftermarket mirrors with side marker blinkers built in.

(Dave Reider photo)

When adding side-view mirrors with built-in blinkers, you'll need some additional wiring work. You'll have to remove your interior door panels and run some wires from the mirror location through the door, avoiding the window's path of movement, into the door grommet along side of the kick panel, and up the underside of the dash where the appropriate connections to the turn signal circuit must be made. Manufacturers provide detailed installation instructions with their mirror kits.

Figure 8.8

This Subaru WRX is sporting a set of carbon fiber racing mirrors. The large opening in the mirror provides functional airflow as well as sharp looks.

(Dave Reider photo)

Mounting Methods

Before you mount anything, make sure the area for mounting is clean and free of dirt. Also, use an alcohol pad to remove any wax or silicone-based product from the surface area. You use both double-sided adhesive tape and screws to mount most lip kits. Use the adhesive tape in the open, visible areas to avoid showing screws; conversely, use screws in the wheel wells as added mounting security.

Figure 8.9

These screws on the side of each fender well provide added security in addition to the double-sided mounting tape to ensure that your side skirt won't come loose.

(Dave Reider photo)

When it comes to mounting body kits, you have several different options. As with side skirts for a lip kit, you usually mount side skirts for a body kit in the same manner. The main difference between mounting a body kit and a lip kit is that for a body kit you will need to unbolt and remove the bumpers and replace the OEM units with the new replacement units; this is simply a remove-and-replace process. Though it may be a bit more time consuming and slightly more difficult, it results in a much better mounting connection since it is being bolted directly into the same factory locations as the original parts were.

Fenders, Doors, and Deck Lids

Okay, now that we've covered hoods, we're going to focus on the other components that open and close, since these also have an impact on how your ride looks.

Weight Versus Strength

Racers have an old saying: "for every one hundred pounds shaved, one hundredth of a second is lost." In the eye of the performance builder, this kind of logic is gospel: the lighter it is, the faster it will go. So what's one to do? Well, if it's speed you're after, you have to put your car on a diet, just as you'd put yourself on one in order to run faster.

Most racers start with the easy stuff, like removing all the sound deadening material. The more dedicated racers may remove interior panels and even the carpet, but what do you do when that's still not enough of a weight savings?

Losing excess weight to gain speed may indeed come down to shaving weight from body panels, but the question here is how much strength are you willing to sacrifice for the weight loss. As discussed earlier, the substitution of carbon fiber components in the tuner world has solved that problem to a large extent. Unlike fiberglass, which used to be the choice of racers, carbon fiber gives the strength needed for safety, yet its light weight can shave significant pounds off your machine. Carbon fiber is an extremely strong material, and the automotive aftermarket industry has taken full advantage of this fact/craze. If you can name it, it is or can be made in carbon fiber. Hoods, bumpers, fenders, doors, deck lids, you name the part, and you can get its steel counterpart made in carbon fiber.

Vented Fenders

Okay, let's talk about vented fenders. Now here's something that has factions on both sides of the fence, as it were. Some will say, "nope, not for me," while others will say, "way cool, I like that." There's a fine line between the two, but that's often the way it is in the tuner world.

Figure 8.10

Here's a Honda Civic with some nice wide-body vented fenders on it.

(Dave Reider photo)

Figure 8.11

The vent openings on these fenders are indeed functional in that they permit the braking system to breathe a bit easier.

(Dave Reider photo)

Many companies make aftermarket fenders both with and without vents. There are also carbon replacement options. Some builders have gone as far as purchasing custom fenders, and then purchasing fender inserts from such brands as BMW, and installing the vents on non-BMW vehicles. The vents, for many, are a styling option. Some builders, however, make them functional so they actually pull air out of the engine bay for cooler running.

Lightweight Doors

Though not recommended for a street car, companies do offer fiberglass or carbon door replacements, again to shave some extra pounds off the weight of their metal counterparts. If you decide to replace your doors, understand that you are compromising your safety since this door is all that stands between you and a side-collision impact, something to give some serious thought to. Many of the newer vehicles that come equipped with side-impact airbags or other safety supports won't be there to offer this protection anymore if you make the exchange. Therefore, this type of modification is only recommended for track cars.

Figure 8.12

How's this for a radical 300M door? Bet even Chrysler never thought of this during their design process!

(Dave Reider photo)

If, however, you do choose to go with a lighter door, the procedure for installation is pretty straightforward. You unbolt the door from the hinges; swap all the internal components from the original door, such as glass, window track, wiring, etc.; and bolt them back onto the replacement door. Some tuners decide to really trick things out by reversing the hinging on their doors, in effect creating *suicide doors*.

You will need to spend some time adjusting how the door sits on the hinges so that it closes properly. Again, having a helper holding your replacement part while you make adjustments is time consuming but makes the process quite a bit easier.

TUNER TALK

Suicide doors refer to doors that are hinged at the rear and open from the front.

Figure 8.13

Check out the Lambo-style form doors and suicide rear doors on this crazy PT Cruiser. Now that's really trick!

(Dave Reider photo)

Lightweight Deck Lids

As with fenders and doors, you can also replace deck lids with fiberglass or carbon fiber units. Many companies make direct replacement units that mount right to your factory hinges using the factory bolts. If your vehicle comes with taillights that are incorporated into the deck lid, be sure the proper accommodations are there on the new deck lid if you intend to use this vehicle on the street; the local law enforcement agents will most assuredly not be happy with your decision to eliminate some important rear lighting! Once again, deck lid replacement is not a one-person job, but it is definitely an easy task with a helper to support the old and new lids as you unbolt and rebolt them into place.

YELLOW FLAG

Remember, too, that if your factory deck lid had any wiring for lighting, you will need to spend a few minutes to reroute that part of the harness accordingly through the aftermarket lid and to the proper locations.

Figure 8.14

This is a nice example of a lightweight carbon fiber aftermarket deck lid on this BMW.

(Dave Reider photo)

Vertical (Scissor) Door Installation

Lambo doors, as they are commonly called, got their name from the pattern of door movement seen on Lamborghinis. Unlike standard cars doors that open outwards, this style of door is hinged to open upward. Quickly adopted as one of the more common stand-out modifications, companies, such as Vertical Doors Inc., have dedicated their entire business solely to this modification genre. Though these kits are advertised as direct bolt-on units (which they actually are), a lot more work is involved to install a set of these.

In many (no, make that most) instances of installing Lambo doors, you must remove the fenders from the vehicle in order to reach the necessary bolts that hold the door hinges to the frame of the ride. And in order to remove the fenders, you will most likely have to remove the front bumper and possibly the headlights, too. You should definitely prepare yourself for this time-consuming project. With a weekend of time to do the work and the right tools, it is not a difficult modification. Essentially, what you will need is patience and proper organization to keep track of what and how you removed everything so that during the reinstall you are not searching for hardware.

Once you have full access to the hinge area, you simply unbolt the factory hinge from the frame and door and replace it on both with the direct bolt-up new hinge system. Of course it will require a few tests and some fine tuning to get everything to close and seat as it should. Then, when both doors are remounted, you'll have the fun task of reinstalling the front end of your car. It will all be worth the effort, however, since the next time you pull up at your local meet, you'll exit your ride in style. And that's really what customizing your ride is all about!

The Least You Need to Know

- ◆ Aftermarket parts are available in urethane, fiberglass, and carbon fiber.

- ◆ Reducing the weight of the vehicle will help to increase its speed.

- ◆ You don't have to purchase complete kits from one manufacturer; you can mix and match as desired.

- ◆ Having helpers makes installing hoods, doors, and deck lids easier.

- ◆ Installing vertical Lambo doors often requires disassembling the front of the vehicle to access the hinge mounting points.

Chapter 9

Fabricating Parts

In This Chapter

- ◆ Working with wood
- ◆ Panels, boxes, and more
- ◆ Molding and mold making
- ◆ Parts of glass for some class

In some instances the component or part you need to achieve a particular look just isn't available as an aftermarket bolt-on piece. For these occasions, you'll need a custom-fabricated part, and making these components usually isn't rocket science, so chances are good that you'll be able to do it yourself with some basic tools. Working with various materials and custom-fabricating parts is what we cover in this chapter, so read on!

Working with Wood

Adding some custom-fabricated woodworking to your car will definitely set it apart and give your ride that one-off touch that will really make it stand out. Although all sorts of aftermarket parts are available, custom-fabricated woodworking really lets you get creative and endow your ride with something totally different from the rest of the crowd. Working with wood may limit you to two-dimensional creations (unless you're really a whiz at whittling); however, wood covered in suede or leather can give your car a clean, sleek, and up-scale finished look.

Wood or Fiberboard

For virtually all of your custom-made projects, you have the choice of using either plywood or medium-density fiberboard (MDF). The choice of which wood composite you use when making trim panels, such as trim around a sub-box, amp, or false floor, doesn't matter as much as how thick the material is. For obvious reasons, you wouldn't want to use quarter-inch-thick board for a false floor; you'd want a much thicker and more durable piece of material for this purpose.

If you're going to make speaker enclosures that will move air, the choice should always be MDF exclusively because it is much denser than either plywood or particle board. Use it for this reason: the denser the board, the less air that can escape; the less air seepage, the better the sound and performance you'll get from your speakers.

As is usually the case, however, better comes at a higher price. Be prepared to pay double the price for MDF as you would for standard plywood in some cases. But rest assured that it is well worth the extra expense in the long run.

Making Trim Panels

Making nice trim panels for your equipment installation is always a great finishing touch. It is fairly common to mount amplifiers onto a wooden back frame and then make a finishing trim plate that gives them a flush-mounted appearance. The advantage to this approach is that no wires or connections are exposed or visible. Only the top heat sink of the unit is seen, resulting in a nice clean, finished look.

The first step in doing this is to make a template or pattern. Use a piece of cardboard to get the overall shape; then transfer the pattern onto the wood, and cut on the outside of the line.

Something to remember here is that it's always better to have the piece be a bit too big because you can always trim it to size a little at a time. Conversely, if the piece is too small, you have to start over again and waste material and time! Woodworkers use an old adage, "Measure twice and cut once." This is good advice that applies here, too.

After you finish the panel outline, the next step is to trace the areas that have to be cut out for the equipment. Depending on your personal taste, you can make these cut-outs to exact size or make them slightly oversized (a ⅛" border all around) so the components can be back-lit with neon to produce a nice glow that surrounds the equipment. Again, your own personal taste will dictate what you do here.

Sub Boxes

You can make subwoofer (subs for short) boxes in an array of styles, including sealed, ported, and bandpass. The sealed enclosure is probably the most commonly used and the easiest to construct. It is simply a rectangular or square box with all its seams sealed with silicone.

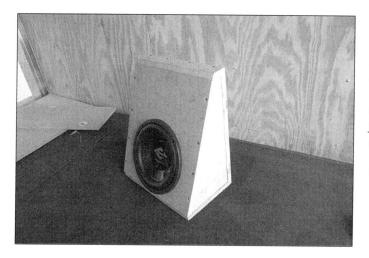

Figure 9.1

This is one of two identical sub boxes designed to fit between the two front seats. The sharp angle of the box is intentional so it won't interfere with the seat's reclining ability.

(Andy Goodman photo)

The speaker(s) airspace requirements and the amount of room you have available for your enclosure will determine whether you can build a box to hold one, two, three, or more subs. Each brand and model of sub has its own space requirements; if the sub is installed in a box that is larger or smaller than what the manufacturer recommends, it will not function properly, and you will have distorted sound.

Figure 9.2

The sub box is undergoing a trial fit here to make sure everything fits as it should before covering it with fabric.

(Andy Goodman photo)

Sealing and Finishing

For assembly, use wood glue on every joint; you can also use it to fill in any gaps or spaces. Be liberal when using it, as you can wipe off any access. You want strong joints here for the best structural integrity.

If your wooden creation is a sub box, carefully seal all the joints, as any open spaces for air to escape will diminish the performance of your subwoofers. As some added insurance, in addition to the wood glue you use for assembly, use silicone (available in tubes at lumber and home improvement centers) on all joints inside the box to guarantee an airtight seal. After applying the glue and silicone, let it cure for at least a day before mounting any equipment in the enclosure. This is a safety measure to protect the subwoofers' composites from the fumes inherent with some glue products. And, because of these fumes, always have adequate ventilation when working with glues and silicone sealants.

Trunk liner material, carpet, vinyl padding, or suede are all great options for coverings because they will help to cover any outer imperfections on the box and also give your box a finished look. Be sure, regardless of the fabric you choose, that the piece is big enough to cover the area with room to spare. It's always infinitely better to trim away any excess material than to have to patch in a piece if you find that your piece is too small.

Use a good quality spray adhesive for mounting the covering fabric, and apply it to both the box and fabric. Give the glue a couple of minutes to set up (get tacky); then place the fabric over the wood. Stretch the fabric slightly when applying it for the best, wrinkle-free fit.

Fiberglass

When using *fiberglass* for custom fabrication work, the only limitations are those you set upon yourself. Though working with fiberglass is, in honesty, a messy and time-consuming process, you can form it into just about any size, shape, or dimension you can imagine.

TUNER TALK

Fiberglass or glassfibre is material made from extremely fine fibers of glass. Used as a reinforcing agent for many polymer products, the resulting composite material, properly known as fiber-reinforced polymers (FRP), is called "fiberglass" in popular usage. What is commonly known as "fiberglass" today, however, was invented in 1938 by Russell Games Slayter of Owens-Corning as a material to be used as insulation.

If you remember back when you were a kid and had to do those messy school projects with paper mache, you can get an inkling of what working with fiberglass is like although it's really quite a bit more involved than paper mache.

Figure 9.3

This fender is going to have an extension flare added to increase its width. The edge of the fender has been stripped down to bare metal to prep for mounting the flare to it with fiberglass.

(Andy Goodman photo)

The process for fabricating with fiberglass is fairly straightforward. First, you make a mold. Next, you lay the "fleece" (fiberglass cloth or matte) into the mold, and seal it with resin to form the basic shape. Then add additional layers of fleece and resin to increase the strength and thickness of the structure or part. When all this is done, you're ready for the finishing steps for this one-off custom item you've made for your ride.

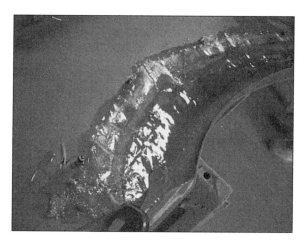

Figure 9.4

Here's the inside of the fender with a healthy coat of fiberglass mesh and resin applied that will serve to strengthen the bond between the fender and the flare.

(Andy Goodman photo)

One of the most appealing things about working with fiberglass is that you can finish it in a number of ways to fit right in with your car's style and theme. Now, let's take a more detailed look at these steps.

Figure 9.5

Now with the inside finished and securely attached, the outside seams are filled in to give the flared fender panel a smooth, finished appearance.

(Andy Goodman photo)

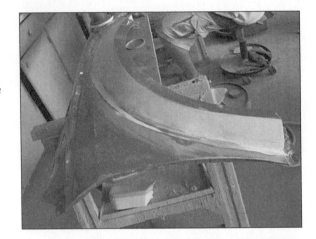

Figure 9.6

The newly-widened fender is remounted to the car, primed and ready for paint. (Andy Goodman photo)

Figure 9.7

Here's the finished product, a custom-made and painted wide-body fender. Fiberglass is indeed a versatile material with a million uses.

(Andy Goodman photo)

Mold Making

You can use several methods to create a mold, the first step in the fiberglass fabrication process. One option is to make a frame out of aluminum foil and/or chicken wire; this works best for free-standing molds. Another option is to make a frame from wood to form the basic outline or skeleton (you can trim the locations where items will be located or mounted later on). With this framework made, stretch the fiberglass cloth over it and apply resin.

Yet another method of creating a mold is to use plastic foam. The advantage of foam is that you can cut and shape it until it is in the exact form you desire. Then apply the glass cloth and resin as with the other methods.

A fourth option is to use an existing shape, for example, the spare tire recess in your trunk, as the basis for your mold.

The method of mold making you decide upon depends largely on what you're fabricating and how industrious and patient you are.

Release Agents

If you choose to use an existing hole, shape, or form, you'll have to use a release agent to remove the original piece from the newly-formed fiberglass part when it is finished or vice-versa.

You can choose several options for release agents. One of the more common choices is 3M blue masking tape; use the blue variety because it doesn't leave a sticky residue when you remove it. Another option is to use a carnauba-based wax which all of today's car care companies produce. There are also PVA (poly vinyl acetate) sprays made specially to be used as release agents, as well as brand-specific products, too.

Gelcoat

Because the newly molded fiberglass part is rarely or never left unfinished and exposed to view, the use of gelcoat is really a moot point, but we're including it here in the interest of completeness. For pieces where the molded surface will be exposed to view or, for some reason, an extremely smooth surface is required, gelcoat is the first layer sprayed or brushed on a mold. One side of that gelcoat layer is in contact with the mold, while the other side gets covered by more resin and cloth layers. Gelcoat is widely used in the boating industry and by mass manufacturers of automotive parts such as fenders and other components that require smooth finishes, but the use of gelcoat is rarely if ever required when fabricating your own custom-made parts. If and when you do need gelcoat, it is available from a variety of manufacturers at boat-building supply houses and some auto body supply houses as well as from mail order suppliers.

Laying Mesh/Glass Cloth

Use the glass cloth or fleece to provide the first nonliquid layer or backbone which the mesh or matt will add strength to. It is a popular but grossly inaccurate misconception that fleece and resin alone will be strong and durable enough to create a viable molded structure. You need to beef things up substantially by adding successive layers to increase strength and thickness.

Once you are satisfied with the structure of your frame, lay the fleece over it, making sure there is plenty of surplus material on all sides. Start in the center and work your way out in a circular motion, stretching the fleece as you staple it down. Once you complete the stapling, apply the first coat of resin. After a few hours of drying time, you will be ready for your first layer of mesh. It's advisable, however, to trim the excess from the edges and cut out any holes necessary to accommodate the equipment before you begin the mesh stage, as it is easier to do the trimming and cutting while the thickness is still relatively thin.

The purpose of the mesh layers is to add strength to the piece. Cut the mesh material into 4" x 4" squares, spread a generous coat of resin on the piece, and lay the mesh pieces in it, overlapping the edges of each piece; then completely cover the mesh with another generous coat of resin. You may have to repeat this procedure for as many as ten layers of mesh depending on how strong you want and need this piece to be.

> ### YELLOW FLAG
> It's always a good idea to wear either disposable latex or nitrile gloves when working with fiberglass cloth and resins to prevent them from making contact with your skin.

The Mix

Similar to working with body filler, fiberglass polymers consist of two components: the resin and the hardener. It takes practice and experience to get the proportions of the mixture just right. Although the manufacturer provides guidelines on the product packaging, there really is no exact measurement, as the ambient temperature and humidity of the environment affect the curing properties of the mixture. Too much hardener and the mixture will dry before you're ready to use it; too little and you could be wasting several hours in between layers waiting for it to cure.

Don't be discouraged. It will take some time before you get the hang of it, but remember that this is a learning process. And don't be surprised if you have to go through several bowls of polymer mixture while you learn the properties of the materials and how variations in the mixture affect it.

> ### IN THE KNOW
> Use a Tupperware or similar flexible bowl for your mixture. The advantage of a flexible bowl is that you can bend and flex it from the outside to crack and release any hardened left-over material when you're finished using it. This permits you to get several uses out of the same bowl.

Filling Gaps

When you are satisfied with the number of layers of mesh you have applied and the overall strength of your enclosure, it's time to fill in any gaps, and for this you'll need to use body filler.

You'll find a number of brands and formulations of body filler available on the shelves of the local auto parts store. The most common is the plastic-based "bondo" type body filler, but other varieties have stranded glass fibers mixed in for additional strength; ultimately, the choice is yours.

Regardless of the brand and formulation, they all have one thing in common. The basic material itself must have a crème hardener added and mixed in for it to harden and set. This hardener is supplied with the can of filler material, and you can purchase additional tubes of hardener separately as needed (you'll probably need additional tubes of hardener to finish off a gallon can of filler).

Generally speaking, a single application of body filler will be sufficient to fill in any gaps or "holidays" in your newly-formed piece. However, in some extreme cases you may have to apply multiple coats to get the shape and curves under control or as smooth as you want them to be. If you intend to paint or upholster the enclosure with some sort of fabric, you need to get it completely finished and as smooth as you can. Focus on the shapes and curves giving them extra attention to make sure they are exactly as you want them to be. You can (and will most likely have to) sand and file in between coats of body filler to smooth and form it as desired. Just be sure it is completely cured (hardened) before you do any abrasive work to it in the forming process.

Finishing

When you are satisfied with the overall appearance of your creation, you are ready for the final, finishing touches. Sometimes color matching your fiberglass pieces to your exterior is a nice touch and helps to bring together the theme of your car. Another popular finish is to cover the pieces in material such as leather, vinyl, Naugahyde, or suede. Be aware, however, that there is a great misconception that fabric can hide any imperfections, but this is definitely not true. The fabric still needs a surface to adhere to, so if the surface has waves or low spots they will be seen through the fabric as well. That's why it's important that you're 100 percent satisfied with the finish of your work before applying fabric to it.

The Least You Need to Know

- Some custom-made wood trim can really make your ride stand out from the rest of the crowd.
- Medium-density fiberboard is the best choice for making speaker enclosures like subwoofer boxes.
- Use WD-40 spray as a release agent, among other things.
- A single layer of fiberglass cloth and resin will not have sufficient strength and rigidity; you'll need multiple layers.
- Any imperfections in the surface of your custom-made fiberglass part or enclosure will still be visible through any fabric covering you use.

Chapter 10

Paint, Graphics, and Glass

In This Chapter

- ◆ Pre-paint preparation
- ◆ Removing parts and masking
- ◆ Special effects and graphics
- ◆ Window tinting and treatments

A killer paint job is what sets the really outstanding rides apart from all the rest, and great paint jobs don't just happen by accident. A lot more goes into producing a really eye-catching paint job than just aiming a spray gun at the car, as you'll soon learn in this chapter.

More than What Meets the Eye

Chances are pretty good that the first thing you notice about any car is its paint job. First, the color attracts the eye, then any graphics or special effects. The power of paint can't and shouldn't be underestimated because it has such a profound impact on the overall appearance of the vehicle. You can have all the trick mods and body kits in the world, but if the paint doesn't immediately grab your eye, it's all for naught. And don't kid yourself; paint won't hide imperfections. To the contrary, it will *accentuate* them.

If something isn't right, it's going to stand out like a sore thumb when you apply paint. And that's a fact, Jack, so now's the time to fix it!

Perfection Is in the Prep

With all other factors being equal, the thing that separates a great paint job from a mediocre one is the amount of preparation that went into it. Preparation, in short, means taking care of everything you need to do for the paint to adhere properly and look its best when you complete the job. While pre-paint preparation is time-consuming, labor-intensive, and, to be honest, mundane and boring; it is absolutely essential if you want your finished paint job to really be killer.

Parts Removal

Essentially, everything that doesn't get painted will have to be masked off or removed from the vehicle. We'll cover masking shortly, but right now let's concentrate on part removal.

Figure 10.1

Emblems, badges, and other small trim parts are frequently held on with "speed" nuts, as shown here with this Corvette emblem. These fasteners are easy to remove and can be reused again to reaffix the trim parts after the painting is completed.

(Tom Benford photo)

Obviously, some parts are easier to remove than others, and because of this you'll have to be selective about which parts you're going to remove prior to applying the paint. Generally speaking, things like emblems, hood ornaments, and headlight and taillight trim are fairly easy to remove because they're usually secured using removable fasteners such as "speed nuts." Other parts such as body side moldings and windshield surround trim can't be easily removed without a substantial amount of skill and special tools, so you're better off leaving these parts on the car. A good rule of thumb is that if you can't get to the fasteners holding the part on or you don't understand how it is fastened, leave it on the car and mask it off rather than remove it.

Dents and Dings

If the car has any body imperfections at all, and that means scratches, dents, pebble-pocks, dings on the doors or anything else that is wrong with the body surface, you must take care of these before you apply paint. If you're experienced at doing body-work, then this is something you can handle right in your own garage. If, on the other hand, you aren't adept at bodywork, you'll want to have an experienced person handle this task. And remember what we said about imperfections earlier; take care of them now, or they'll be back to bite you on the eye after the paint is dry!

Figure 10.2

This Scion is all ready to be masked and painted after sanding and body work have been finished.

(Andy Goodman photo)

Masking

As noted earlier, if you can't remove the parts you don't want painted, you must mask them off so paint won't get on them. As with every other aspect of paint prep, the better the job of masking, the better the end result will be. Use only high-quality auto-motive masking tape (available at the local auto parts supply store or body shop supply house); the adhesive on the tape you find at the stationary supply store isn't formulated to withstand the solvents and fumes in automotive paints, so it won't adhere properly, and overspray will get on areas that you don't want painted.

In addition to using the right kind of tape, do a good job applying the tape. You want to completely isolate masked areas from paint spray, and applying the masking tape properly is essential for this purpose. You can even get masking tape with masking paper already attached to one side of it, which is a big help in masking off larger areas. This tape/paper masking is also available at body shop supply stores and better auto parts centers.

Figure 10.3

Here's the Scion with priming and the color coat applied. Notice how thoroughly the engine compartment and other areas protected from paint have been carefully masked off to prevent overspray.

(Andy Goodman photo)

For large areas, such as windshields, side windows, and inner fender wells that you don't want painted, use several thicknesses of newspaper or brown craft paper to shield against paint overspray.

The more time you spend carefully masking, the less time you'll have to spend removing paint from unwanted areas. Of the two, masking is definitely the easier job!

Priming

Primer is the first paint coat that goes on the vehicle, and it is applied, like other automotive finishes, in a paint booth. One of the main reasons for using a paint booth is because the booth keeps paint vapors and byproducts from escaping into the atmosphere. It also keeps atmospheric artifacts, such as dust, pollen, and soot, from entering the booth and settling onto the painted surface of the vehicle. Obviously, your garage doesn't have this kind of filtration technology to keep this stuff out, so it is far from an ideal setting for painting your ride.

IN THE KNOW

The EPA (Environmental Protection Agency) has strict guidelines regarding the use of automotive finishes, and licensed auto body repair facilities are required under law to comply with these guidelines. One of the mandates is an approved paint booth. The purpose of the paint booth is to contain the vapors and overspray produced when painting a vehicle and prevent this stuff from entering the atmosphere. It is illegal to spray outside a paint booth. For this reason, you really don't want to spray your ride in your garage and break the law, do you?

And also consider this. Automotive paints have powerful odors; in fact, they stink, to be blunt. You're not going to be voted Best Citizen on the Block once your neighbors get a whiff of this noxious-smelling stuff emanating from your garage, and you'll be even less popular when the breeze carries overspray particles out into the neighborhood, settling all over the place. Nope, you better rethink this whole "I'll paint it myself in the old garage" thing, for sure.

Having said that, the purpose of priming is to give the vehicle a foundation surface the outer paint layers can adhere to. Priming also serves to smooth out slight (and we mean really slight) imperfections in the surface and to make the overall surface to be painted more uniform. For high-end paint jobs, it is not at all uncommon to apply several coats of primer, with wet-sanding performed between coats.

Applying Color

As with priming, applying color coats is subject to the same cautions and warnings as applying primer.

Today's automotive finishes give you quite a few options. The most basic scenario is the simple color coat, topped off with clear coat to give it luster and shine. But you also have more involved options when it comes to applying finish color(s) to your ride.

YELLOW FLAG

Automotive finishes contain chemicals, vapors, and particles not meant to be taken into human respiratory systems. Therefore, using these materials without taking the proper precautions and wearing the correct protective gear is foolish and dangerous. Wearing a respirator when using these materials is an absolute must!

Multistage finishes consist of applying a base coat (usually a silver or gold base) over the primer, then shooting a translucent color coat over the base. This results in a rich, "candy" color finish. If you've ever seen "candy apple red," then you know what we're talking about here. But there's even more than simple base/color/clear multistage finishes.

Figure 10.4

Attention to detail is the rule of the day for a winning paint job. Leave no crevices unpainted as illustrated here showing that even the inside of the gas cap door has been sprayed.

(Andy Goodman photo)

You can elect to have pearl powders added to the color or even clear coats to endow the paint with chameleon-like characteristics that will cause it to change color when viewed from different angles or as the ambient lighting changes.

Other special effects you can apply with paint include "ghost" images, such as flames or other visuals that only become visible from certain angles or under certain lighting conditions. So indeed, you have many choices for the overall look of your ride, not just the basic color choices.

Clear Coating

Clear coating is, as the name implies, a coating of clear paint that adds luster and depth to the paint underneath. Clear coat paint usually has chemicals added to it to give it some flexibility and resistance to chipping. It's helpful to think of clear coating as a protective wrapping for your paint because it protects the actual color coats underneath it. If the clear coating is thick enough, you can buff out surface nicks and scratches without affecting the color coats. For this reason, having several coats of clear over your color coats is advisable. As with primer, wet sanding between clear coats produces the best finish overall. And this brings us to our next topic.

Sanding and Buffing

Both sanding and buffing are processes that remove unwanted material. When spray painting, unwanted byproducts are always deposited on the paint surface. Most of the time this is just a build-up of spray that gives a slightly irregular surface called "orange peel" (which pretty much describes what it looks like). To eliminate the "orange peel" and any stray dust particles that may settle on the paint before it is thoroughly dry, sanding is done as part of the overall finishing process.

Though it is indeed time-consuming and labor-intensive, careful and thorough *wet sanding* is well worth the effort. It pays off big dividends by giving you a finished paint job that is absolutely gorgeous. When you perform all the pre- and post-painting steps correctly, the end paint job looks like it is under glass.

> **TUNER TALK**
>
> **Wet sanding** is usually performed on painted surfaces, regardless of whether they are primer coats, color coats, or clear coats. A very fine grit of sandpaper, usually 400 grit or better (600 grit is the norm), dipped in water, is used to sand the painted surface. The water serves as a lubricant and also washes away the waste material removed by the sanding; hence, the name "wet sanding."

Buffing with a lamb's wool buffing wheel and a micro-fine polishing liquid is the true finishing touch to bring out the deepest luster and shine of the finished paint job. Investing in a good electric buffer is worthwhile for freshening up your car's paint before a big meet or show, and it's also great for buffing out small scratches in the clear coat.

Paint Effects

As mentioned earlier, you can add all sorts of special effects when painting your ride. In addition to the pearl and "ghost" effects, you can cross-fade one color into another, have "shredding" effects applied so it looks like the paint is peeling off from sheer speed, add airbrushed graphics of just about any description you can imagine as well as pin striping, a paint effect as old as customizing itself. As with all other things in the customizing bag of tricks, the choice is strictly up to you and what you want your ride to look like. Of course, looking at what others have done is always a good place to start, taking good ideas and modifying them to your own tastes and preferences.

Figure 10.5

Nice, clean graphics can definitely add a touch of class to any ride. They don't have to be complex, just tasteful and well-placed.

(Dave Reider photo)

Vinyl Graphics/Decals

Increasingly popular and a great way to individualize your ride is the use of vinyl graphics and decals. Although the assortments of ready-made, ready-to-apply graphics and decals is extensive, for a truly one-of-a-kind look you might want to design something yourself and have it transferred into a vinyl pattern or decal by a local sign shop or custom paint shop.

Figure 10.6

It's really hard to beat a well-done airbrushed graphic when it comes to grabbing attention. Here's an excellent example of what we mean.

(Andy Goodman photo)

If you don't have sufficient artistic prowess yourself, you can always ask a friend who does to sketch out your idea as you describe it to him or her, and then have the sketch made into a transfer.

Window Tinting and Treatments

Window tinting consists of applying a thin film to the stock glass of your car. This keeps some of the sun's rays out of your cabin and also creates a bit more privacy for you and your passengers. Additionally, window tinting will help to increase the longevity of your vehicle's interior in several ways. Tint prevents those nasty ultraviolet rays that are the leading cause of interior fading from entering; tint also helps to keep some heat out of your car during those hot summer months. And window tint is also a preventive blocker against the demons that dry out your leather seats and cause cracking. Be aware, however, that although tint serves many useful purposes, it can also be illegal once it meets or exceeds a certain shade of darkness.

Shade Versus Color Tinting

Two types of tinting film exist. The first is what we call privacy tint. Offered by companies, such as Llumar, in several shades, the most popular standard tints are 70 percent, 50 percent, 35 percent, 20 percent, and 5 percent. These numbers represent the amount of natural light that still comes through the tint film. In other words, 70 percent tint is on the lighter side of the scale because it allows 70 percent of the natural light to come through; conversely, 5 percent is the darkest as it only allows 5 percent of the natural light to penetrate.

The other common variation of window tint is similar to that of standard tint except it is colored. Companies, such as Gila, produce tint in an array of colors including, but not limited to, yellow, red, and blue. Be advised that these tints are not street legal and are meant for show purposes only, but they are definitely eye-catchers when trying to make your car stand out from the rest. Another important factor to consider when deciding on what shade to go with is your car's interior color. The darker the interior, the darker the tint will look. For example if you put 20 percent tint on a white interior vehicle and 35 percent on a black interior vehicle, it will be difficult to tell the difference between the two.

YELLOW FLAG

Be careful and learn your state's laws before purchasing tint. Each and every state across America has different laws as to what is street legal and what is for show use only. Knowing what's legal and what's not may be the difference between getting a ticket and getting a trophy.

Windshield Strips

A windshield strip is just what it sounds like, a strip that goes across the top of the windshield. For obvious safety reasons it is highly illegal to tint the entire front windshield. However, a small strip that descends a few inches from the top of your windshield to help shade you from the sun's direct rays is permissible.

How do you know how far down to go? Well, you probably never even noticed it, but on most newer vehicles on both sides of the windshield approximately three to five inches from the top on the far edges you'll see a small line, scarcely an inch in length if even that long. This line signifies the lowest you can go legally with a windshield strip. Some cars come from the factory with extra ultra violet protection in this area in the form of a UV blocker; however, because it is built into the glass itself, it's nothing to worry about as you can apply a windshield strip right over it without a problem.

Side Windows

After deciding what type of tint treatment is right for you, the question becomes which windows to tint and which to leave untinted. Knowing the front windshield is out of the question other than for a windshield strip, you need to ask yourself about the others. Most folks want to maintain a consistent flow throughout the car and tint the sides and rear window all the same shade, although it is also quite common to leave the two front windows untinted for clearer visibility. Another common option is to make the rear window lighter than the sides so rear vision isn't hindered. Again, the decisions are up to you.

Applying Window Tint

Window tinting is a DIY (do it yourself) job, and it's easy to do with the right tools; a sharp blade, a plastic squeegee, and a squirt bottle are all you need. The tinting film comes in a roll that you can purchase at any automotive retail chain.

First, establish which side of the film is the inside that goes on the window. Then thoroughly clean both the inside and outside of the glass. Next spray liberal amounts of your solution on the outside of the glass; don't worry about it running, it won't stain anything.

Now place the film on the outside of the glass with the removable plastic protective coating facing you. Then carefully cut the film, tracing the inside lines of your glass. Next, spray your solution on the inside of the window, peel back the protective coating, and place the tint carefully on the inside of the window. Position the film by hand, and then, working from the center of the window outward, begin to force the excess water out using the squeegee.

You have to be careful here. Don't push too hard, or you will scratch the tint; on the other hand, don't push too lightly, or the tint won't adhere properly. Follow these same procedures for each window, and when you're finished, you'll have a tinted vehicle.

IN THE KNOW

When preparing your squirt bottle, fill it with water, and put in two or three drops of general dish detergent. The added soap will make the solution more slippery, which makes working with the tint easier.

One final thing to remember as far as tinting goes: after tinting your windows, leave your windows in the up position for three to four days (or even longer in the winter months) to let the tinting film dry thoroughly against the glass. If it isn't thoroughly dry, lowering your window can cause a mishap, and you certainly don't want to have to tint it again!

Glass Engraving

Although glass engraving was once in vogue with the "old school" customizers and has always been a favorite treatment of the *low-rider* people, it never really caught on with the mainstream modern tuner crowd. Note we used the word mainstream here; engraving was, has been, and probably will continue to be popular with customizers (yes, we're talking about tuner people here) who listen to the beat of their own individual drummer. To them we say, "Go for it." After all, making your ride an individual statement of what you like and what you think is cool is what it's all about, and if that includes glass engraving, more power to you!

Low-riders are cars that have had their suspensions lowered to the point where the bodies almost scrape the ground. Low-riders are very popular with Latino car buffs in Southern California where low-riders first originated. These cars will frequently have hydraulically-controlled suspensions that permit them to raise and lower very rapidly and even "dance" by causing the car to jump up and down by inflating and deflating the suspension.

The Least You Need to Know

◆ The best paint jobs begin with the best pre-paint preparation.

◆ Removing parts you don't plan to paint is often better than masking them off.

◆ Automotive paints and associated chemicals have vapors that are harmful to your lungs.

◆ Painting a vehicle without a paint booth is a violation of EPA mandates and can get you in serious trouble.

◆ Dark tint shades may be illegal in your state, so check local laws before applying tint.

Part 4

Performance–
Packing More Ponies

While it's great to be able to "talk the talk," it's even better if you can "walk the walk," too! So that's what we're up to in this section—you can show the world that your ride is more than just a pretty face—it's got the brawn to back up its beauty, too.

You've got a lot of latitude when it comes to packing some extra punch under the hood—you can go mild, wild, or totally gonzo-aggressive—it's all up to you how far you want to take it. But regardless of which stop you want to get off at while riding the performance bus, we'll tell you exactly what you'll need and how to get it.

All you've got to remember is that you need four things to make your ride a real screamer: air, fuel, and spark … What's the fourth thing, you ask? That's simple—you and your desire to make it quicker! So, come on—turn the key and let's crank up the ponies!

Fire in the Hole (Hotter Ignition)

In This Chapter

- ◆ Ignition parts
- ◆ Plugs and wires
- ◆ Coils and coil packs
- ◆ Ignition modules

The ignition system can really be called the heart of the engine because it literally provides the spark of life. While many people are mystified and often intimidated by ignition systems, they really aren't hard to understand. And once you understand how they work, getting more out of them becomes a relatively easy task. That's what we're up to in this chapter, squeezing more horses out of the ignition system.

Turning Up the Heat

The primary job of the ignition system is to ignite the fuel. However, the ignition system must work in perfect harmony with the rest of the motor, or the result will be a power loss and excessive gas consumption.

In the world of aftermarket accessories, hundreds of products are available to help better control and maximize the ignition systems optimum spark, and many of these goodies add an appreciable amount of *eye candy* under the hood, too. Today's technology far surpasses what was available to past generations with regard to increasing ignition performance and efficiency. Thanks to computers and high-tech programs, we can now fine-tune an ignition system to produce the utmost efficiency. And we can do this right from a laptop or notebook PC!

> **TUNER TALK**
>
> **Eye candy** refers to anything special, attractive, or particularly eye-catching on a vehicle, especially under the hood items.

Ignition Components

Though the ignition system in any car may sound complex at first blush, breaking it down and taking it on a component-by-component basis makes it easy to understand. At the heart of the ignition system is the coil, and this is really where it all begins. The coil amplifies the voltage coming from the battery and passes it through a high-voltage wire to the distributor which, as the name implies, distributes this high-energy voltage through wires to each spark plug. This plug, in turn, ignites the air/fuel mixture in the cylinder that produces the power. Still sound complicated? Okay, we'll break it down a bit more so it's easier to digest.

The distributor is an assembly made up of several components: the distributor body, a cam, a rotor, and a distributor cap. We should mention that some vehicles don't actually have a distributor but use coil packs instead. These serve as both the coil and the means of power distribution. But anyway, let's get back to the distributor.

Inside the distributor cap, a cam rotates (governed by the engine timing system); this turns the rotor, which makes contact with terminals connected to each spark plug wire. As the rotor turns and makes contact, the high-voltage passes through the wire connected to the spark plug terminal and makes contact at the opposite end, causing the plug to generate the spark that ignites the fuel.

Each and every component is crucial to proper operation of the ignition system; if there is a problem with any one of these components, the vehicle will not function properly or may not even start. Upgrading some or all of these components will make the engine more efficient on a performance level but, even more importantly, on a gas consumption level. An engine running at top efficiency produces more power and uses less fuel.

All Plugs Are Not Created Equal

Consider the spark plug: this little component fits easily in the palm of your hand, and yet it's one of the most crucial components to an engine. A spark plug forces electricity to arc across a gap, much like watching lightning in the sky. Most factory spark plugs are quite simple affairs with a single electrode on the tip that produces the electrical arc. You can, however, upgrade to higher-performance plugs, which is a simple modification to make using a basic ratchet and socket set.

When thinking of doing a spark plug upgrade, consider these choices. First, decide whether to go with a premium long life or indium plug. These plugs, though a little more costly, can and do perform better under hotter requirements and also last longer than their stock counterparts.

IN THE KNOW

Indium is an element (its atomic number is 49) used to coat the electrodes of premium-performance spark plugs. It is reputed to be up to eight times stronger and more electrically conductive than platinum.

Another choice is going to a high-end performance plug. These are the most costly, but their unique configurations and multiple electrode edges increase spark exposure to the fuel mixture that results in better and more efficient spark.

IN THE KNOW

Changing your spark plugs right before the winter months will help to ensure smoother starts for your car when extreme cold weather hits. There's nothing like having a nice, hot spark to get you off to a fast, clean start!

Better Plug Wires

The spark plug wires transfer the power from the coil packs or distributor to the proper cylinder and cause the plug to fire. We've all experienced that "bogged down" feeling when we stepped on the accelerator at one time or another, right? The main reason this happens is this: as you give your car more gas, the engine needs more spark to ignite and burn that gas. But with small, inefficient wires to carry that all-important high-voltage current, the plugs don't get the power they need to produce a spark that's up to the higher demand they're being put under. A good analogy here is to think of the plug wire as a garden hose and the electrical current coming from the distributor as a golf ball. No matter how hard you try, you can't get the golf ball to fit in and travel down that hose; it's just not going to happen.

It's a similar situation with your stock plug wires: you can't force more power through them than they are capable of carrying. Stock wires are usually 7.5mm thick; you can upgrade to 8mm or even 9mm wires and the result is better performance and fuel economy. Swapping out the old wires for better high-performance wires is simply an easy pull-off, push-on exchange.

Figure 11.1

These sets of custom spark plug wires are ready for purchase on the rack at a tuner show.

(Dave Reiter photo)

Another benefit of upgraded sparkplug wires is that they are much better insulated than stock wires; this is a really big plus for you automotive audio and video fans because the beefed-up insulation will eliminate (or significantly reduce) feedback or engine whine coming through your speakers. (We return to these feedback/whine issues in a later chapter.)

Figure 11.2

This Saturn is sporting custom color-coordinated aftermarket plug wires for extra under-hood eye appeal.

(Dave Reiter photo)

Hotter Coils

As mentioned earlier, we call the ignition component that creates the high voltage necessary to produce the proper spark the *coil*.

The primary coil first amplifies the electrical current coming from the battery and then passes it on to the secondary coil which amplifies it even more. The current then travels on to the distributor for distribution to the spark plugs via the plug wires.

Companies, such as MSD, make upgraded ignition coils that are capable of producing more voltage by utilizing more powerful internal components to promote better electrical conductivity. Because the coil is the first component in the overall ignition process, it is the most crucial component of the ignition system. If your coil doesn't have the proper conductivity to amplify the energy needed to send adequate voltage through the wires and into the spark plugs, you will not have enough spark to efficiently ignite the fuel and less-than-ideal combustion will result. In everyday English, this translates into power loss.

> **TUNER TALK**
>
> The **coil** is a simple device made up of two coils of wire. The first or primary coil is in the center, surrounded by the outer or secondary wire coil, which is much longer and wraps around the center coil.

By upgrading the coil to a more efficient unit, you can generate more energy for the spark plugs, resulting in better ignition. Now, this is all well and good. But remember what we said earlier: if you don't have the proper wires to carry it and high-performance plugs to accept it, this additional power generated by the upgraded coil will be of no use and can actually damage other stock ignition components. Therefore, if you're going to upgrade the ignition system, take a holistic approach.

Ignition Modules Demystified

Many companies produce aftermarket ignition modules that *piggyback* on your factory wiring or have to be hard-wired into the ignition circuit. Although these aftermarket modules used to be the best way to get more spark on older engines, with current motor technology that isn't always the case.

Today's technology has progressed and advanced to the point that, thanks to the built-in engine computer controls, external ignition modules really aren't necessary anymore. Essentially, you can control all of the same functions and achieve the same end results by changing the timing and reprogramming your vehicles computer (which we'll get to shortly). Upgrading the vehicle's plug wires and coil will make all the difference for high-output performance street machines. In actuality, for an everyday street machine or occasional track run, installing a secondary ignition module will not make your ride perform any better.

> **TUNER TALK**
>
> A **piggyback** is any electronic item that plugs in between components that are connected through your factory wiring harness. No additional wiring is necessary, so in effect, a piggyback component is literally "plug and play."

Notice we said "everyday street machine or occasional track run"; that's the distinction here. Now, if you have a nine-second track car, and you're determined to squeeze out every single ounce of energy and want to make sure right down to the very last millisecond that everything fires properly from your ignition system, well, then yes, an aftermarket ignition module will probably help your engine's operation a bit. But in everyday driving situations, you'd never notice the difference one iota.

The Least You Need to Know

- ◆ Several crucial components that include the coil, distributor or coil pack, plug wires, and spark plugs make up the ignition system.
- ◆ High-energy ignitions require high-performance spark plug wires to deliver the current efficiently to the spark plugs.

- Changing spark plug wires and spark plugs is an easy modification to make that will produce more power and greater fuel economy.

- Using a notebook computer, you can reprogram today's modern engines to change their timing and tuning.

- No aftermarket ignition module will produce any noticeable performance increases in everyday driving situations.

Chapter 12

Deep Breathing (Air Induction)

In This Chapter

- ◆ Air filters
- ◆ Cold air and ram air
- ◆ Superchargers
- ◆ Turbochargers

For internal combustion to take place in an engine, three elements are essential: spark, air, and fuel. In the last chapter we covered the importance of the ignition system, which produces the spark. Now let's look at the next crucial element: air and how to get more of it into the engine for increased performance. So take a deep breath, and let's get right to it!

More Air = Bigger Bang

Just as increasing the spark enhances engine performance, so, too, does increasing the amount of air the engine ingests. Indeed, increasing the amount of air has a direct effect on increasing the power output and also helps the engine run more efficiently.

By decreasing the restrictions that limit the flow of air and by bringing colder air into the motor, you help your motor's operation significantly. However, we don't want to give you the impression that you're going to be thrown back in your seat when you step on the gas after making these air induction mods. The truth is you may only wind up with a handful of increased ponies as the payoff. However, all the little improvements we're suggesting are reasonable in cost and, when you put them all together, the potential power increase can indeed be significant—and noticeable.

Replacement Air Filters

Absolutely the easiest way to ease some air restriction is by purchasing and installing aftermarket direct replacement air filters. Companies, such as K&N Filters, make direct replacements for most of today's popular vehicles.

Figure 12.1

This is what a typical drop-in replacement looks like in the package. It's an easy and inexpensive way to help your engine breathe easier.

(Dave Reider photo)

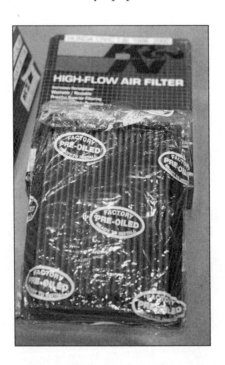

Installation is easy and only requires replacing your stock paper filter with the new direct-fit aftermarket filter. There is no cutting or drilling involved. Simply put the new filter in place of the old one.

Though more costly than their stock *OEM* counterparts, not only will your vehicle breathe better with high-performance aftermarket filters, but filters from some companies, such as K&N, last forever. Instead of replacing your stock filter every few thousand miles as recommended by the vehicle manufacturer, you only have to clean some of these aftermarket filters as recommended and drop them right back into place. You'll never have to buy another replacement air filter again, so they'll save you some bucks in the long run.

TUNER TALK

OEM is an abbreviation for Original Equipment Manufacturer, or, in other words, "stock" parts that come from the factory.

Figure 12.2

This is a stock Scion TC air box—not much to look at, right?

(Dave Reider photo)

Figure 12.3

Now here's the Scion with an aftermarket breather installed. Some difference over stock, isn't it?

(Dave Reider photo)

Cold Air Packages

The air intake, as we refer to it here, is the piece connected to your engine that lets in air via a filter and some tubing or piping. Once air is within the air intake, it flows to the intake manifold which inducts the air into the engine.

Figure 12.4

Check out the nicely-polished pipe work on this air intake tube. It never hurts to have some additional bling under the hood.

(Dave Reider photo)

The "cold air intake" draws cold air in from somewhere else other than the engine bay because air outside the engine compartment is bound to be colder than the air circulating around the engine itself under the hood.

If you look at any engine, you will see that stock air intake piping leads to the filter located inside the engine bay. So what happens here is that all this hot air surrounding the engine gets pulled into the engine. While this isn't the worst thing in the world, it isn't the most efficient way to foster combustion, either. Cold air helps atomize and burn the fuel much more efficiently than hot air does. Do the math here for yourself: cold air = more efficient combustion = more power.

Many aftermarket companies have devised cold air intake systems. These aftermarket kits are direct bolt-in applications that actually relocate the filter outside the engine bay. Oh, so you want to know *where* outside the engine bay, huh? Well, usually this relocation moves the filter to the open space between your inner and outer fender well. This allows the filter to pick up fresh, cooler air to help your engine run more efficiently. Installing these kits doesn't take long and usually requires only basic tools.

Ram-Air Kits

A few chapters back we told you about ram-air hoods. The purpose of a ram-air hood is to force air into the engine bay, which is good, but it's only one part of the overall equation. The ram-air kit is the second part of that equation.

In a ram-air system, piping is required to direct the air into the engine. This piping is either included when you purchase the hood, or you can purchase it as an option. The effect is that as the air hits your hood, it gets scooped up and sent right into your motor at a much greater force than it would normally enter the engine. The way this type of system usually works is that the piping runs from the opening in the hood to an in-line air filter and then through more piping to the intake manifold. Thus the system forces more air into the motor at a greater rate of flow. The denser the air when it reaches the motor, the more efficient the fuel burn will be and the more power the engine will generate.

Intake-to-Throttle Body Kits

An intake-to-throttle body kit is similar to a cold air intake kit except that in this type of system you change the piping all the way to the throttle body. This is generally considered the most efficient type of aftermarket intake system available because, by changing all the plumbing to less-restrictive, more direct piping, you give the air a better channel to flow through.

These ram-air kits are make-and-model specific, not the generic type of mod you can just go to the corner hardware store and buy for any car. You really need to purchase the correct replacement for your specific vehicle. Because the engine bays in today's cars are usually so tight, many times the piping has to follow a specific path or channel, so a kit designed expressly for your make and model is an absolute must.

> **IN THE KNOW**
>
> Stock intake tubing is usually rough and can have harsh bends at some points. Using a metal or carbon tube that is completely smooth alleviates any restrictions on the air flow, thus helping your engine to breathe a lot easier.

Installations and Maintenance

Installing virtually any type of air intake system is a DIY project that you can do with some basic tools in just a few hours. First, carefully remove the old unit. To do so, you need to locate any and all sensors that run to your factory system, then carefully remove the sensors by backing out whatever screws or nuts hold them down. It generally isn't necessary to unplug anything unless it's in the way and disconnecting it makes it easier for you to work; usually, however, you can just move anything out of the way without unplugging.

Next, find where the stock mounting points are, and disconnect those fasteners; often you'll find one or two support brackets attached to the frame of your car. When these are encountered, just be attentive and check everything, especially where they are located and what they attach to; each vehicle is different. When you've disconnected everything, remove the whole unit and set it down somewhere out of the way.

Before attempting to install the new unit, fully read all the instructions and make sure you understand them. The aftermarket kit should bolt right back into the factory mounting points using the original factory hardware.

Next, reinstall any sensors you have removed, but again, your new system will have the necessary mounting points to accommodate them as well. Then attach your new filter just as you did with your old intake system.

Reputable and nationally-known companies, such as K&N Filters, guarantee their filters up to one million miles. So it's a pretty safe bet that no matter how well you take care of your ride, the filter will outlast it by a long shot if you maintain it properly.

Maintenance on an aftermarket filter is usually quite easy. Many times all you need to do is to remove it, rinse it, let it dry, and put it back in the car. K&N Filters has also devised a recharge kit that contains recharging oil you spray on the filter after cleaning it that makes it perform like new.

Forced Induction (Superchargers and Turbo Kits)

If you really want to kick your performance up several notches, then you'll want to consider a supercharger or a turbocharger. Both of these performance-enhancing devices can cost a considerable amount of money, but for many folks the increased performance they deliver by significantly increasing engine *RPM* justifies the cost.

TUNER TALK

RPM is an abbreviation for revolutions per minute and it generally refers to the rotational speed of an engine's crankshaft. Tachometers measure engine RPM and have a red line on them, designating the upper safe limit an engine can be pushed to. Exceeding the red line is courting disaster, as the engine may simply self-destruct from being pushed beyond its structural and engineering limits.

Superchargers and How They Work

The easiest and perhaps the clearest way to define a supercharger is to call it an engine-driven air pump. Pulleys and a belt drive the supercharger, which is powered by the rotation of the engine's crankshaft. The supercharger compresses and forces air into the intake manifold, thereby substantially increasing the volume of air that mixes with the fuel. The end result is a substantial increase in power resulting from the more powerful explosions occurring within the cylinders. The amount of increased air pressure generated by the supercharger and supplied to the engine is called "boost."

Figure 12.5

Here's a great example of a super-clean supercharger installation, with all the goodies sporting beautiful chrome plating.

(Dave Reider photo)

A supercharger (also called a *blower*) provides its additional power boost only when you step on it, not when you're just cruising. Therefore, under normal driving conditions, a supercharger will not affect the engine's fuel economy, longevity, or reliability.

Right now we are going to put to rest a major myth about superchargers. Many people think superchargers are bad for your motor and can blow your engine up because they are too powerful. This is not, by itself, true. Engine damage is usually caused by excessive RPM. Since superchargers are intended to produce more power at lower RPM, supercharged engines are actually more efficient

TUNER TALK

Blower is a slang term used to denote a supercharger. Likewise, saying a motor is "blown" means it is super-charged; but don't confuse this with a motor that has blown up!

than their naturally-aspirated (nonsupercharged) counterparts. All of this is true, of course, with the understanding that they are used within the parameters suggested by their manufacturers. Over-revving a supercharged motor, or even a nonsupercharged motor, for that matter, will have a bad outcome, for sure.

Turbochargers and How They Work

Turbochargers, frequently called "turbos" for short, are also devices for forcing induction. They are similar in concept and function to the supercharger, except for the way they are powered. As we stated earlier, superchargers are belt driven by pulleys and powered by the engine's rotational energy. Conversely, turbochargers are powered by the flow of exhaust gases that spin a turbine which, in turn, powers the air pump.

Figure 12.6

This Ford Focus is benefiting from the added horsepower the Roush turbocharger delivers.

(Dave Reider photo)

Aside from the differences in how each device is powered, their functions are identical: to compress and force more air into the intake manifold for the purpose of producing additional power in the combustion chambers.

A turbocharger gets bolted to the exhaust manifold of the engine and uses those expelled exhaust gases as the powering force to spin the internal turbine. As the turbine spins on one side, its opposite side picks up fresh air, compresses it, and sends it into the motor. Hence, the more exhaust released from a turbocharged vehicle, the faster the turbine spins and the more boost it creates. Now that's what we call recycling where it matters!

Turbochargers need exhaust gases to produce power, so they begin functioning from the moment you start your engine. However, the power they produce is directly proportional to the harder your motor itself works. In other words, the harder your motor works, the more exhaust gasses it produces, so the faster the turbine spins and the more functional the turbo becomes. If you've ever seen the mythological symbol of a serpent swallowing its own tale, that's a good analogy of what's going on here with a turbocharger.

Figure 12.7

For those with an insatiable hunger for power, here's a brand new turbo, fresh out of the box and ready to install. That should make your mouth water!

(Dave Reider photo)

Okay, so turbochargers sound wonderful, don't they? After all, they use the exhaust gases that are produced anyway, but they recycle them into useful and usable power. But as with every other benefit, there's a downside, and the downside here is something called "turbo lag." This term simply identifies the time interval (or lag) that occurs when the turbine goes from just idling up to the speed when it is actually creating usable boost. Depending on the turbo itself as well as the engine it's installed on, this can range from almost instantaneous to a few seconds before the boost actually kicks in.

Adding a turbocharger to any vehicle is really an art and a science because a lot of variables are involved. You just can't pick up the biggest one you see and slap it on your engine; you have to know what size turbo will work properly with your vehicle. On the bright side, however, dozens of major manufacturers have already removed the physics end of the equation for you. Companies, such as Greddy and HKS, make complete everything-you-need kits, but make sure you buy the correct kit. It is absolutely essential that you know your car's motor and drive train specifics before you research and purchase a forced induction system for it.

Figure 12.8

Well, if one turbocharger is good, then two of them have to be better, right?

(Dave Reider photo)

Making the Right Choice

Superchargers and turbochargers are both great additions to any vehicle as either device can potentially increase the motor's power output by as much as 40 percent or more. In objectively comparing both side by side, both have their strong and weak points. (What's that? You didn't think superchargers had a downside? Read on.)

Let's talk dollars first, since money is usually the main ingredient when it comes to increasing performance. Comparing the two on average, a supercharger kit will usually be cheaper than it's turbo counterpart for the same vehicle. However, though it may cost less, a supercharger will add more weight to the engine than a turbocharger will. And, if you recall, less weight means more speed; the heavier the burden, the harder the engine has to work and the slower the vehicle moves.

Now, let's talk performance differences. A supercharger kicks as soon as you punch it, which means to really step on the gas. It's better for a driver who likes to get off the line quicker. A supercharger will kick in harder and be the better bet for you if you are the kind of driver who likes serious acceleration from a dead stop. A turbo, on the other hand, is better for the driver who wants to feel a decided improvement over the full RPM scale. Even though a turbo isn't as powerful as a supercharger off the line, it will increase the power output by spreading it throughout the whole RPM range, rather than just on initial acceleration. The choice is, once again, a matter of personal preference.

Bolt-On Installations

Installing a forced induction system, whether it's a turbocharger or a supercharger, can be a DIY task provided you have the right tools and are willing to devote a full weekend to labor. In truth, the average system takes about eight hours to install, but always give yourself extra time as you should never rush perfection. This is especially true if you've never done this sort of thing before.

Regardless of which style of forced induction system you purchase, the very first thing to do is to inventory all the components that come with the kit against the instructions to make absolutely sure everything you need is right in front of you. Take it from the voice of experience here; the last thing you want to do is get three quarters of the way finished with the installation and find out you're missing a specific bracket that is absolutely necessary for your car to function at its full capacity.

The kit can and should come with all the necessary brackets, hardware, piping, and accessories you need to perform the installation, but just double check all of this to be on the safe side. Take your time to read the instructions, and then read them again! Then proceed with the installation step by step. Some of the higher end kits come complete with the necessary upgraded injector fuel pump and other needed components because as you add more air into your engine, you need to compensate for it by adding more fuel and spark, too.

Increasing performance is rarely, if ever, a single-step operation. Truly impressive performance increases are the result of taking a holistic approach; everything is proportionately upgraded to work with all of the other components harmoniously and to best advantage.

The Least You Need to Know

- More air entering the combustion chamber produces better combustion.
- Cold air increases combustion efficiency.
- The more efficient the combustion is, the more power it produces along with better fuel economy.
- Installing virtually any cold air kit or package is a do-it-yourself project that doesn't require special tools and takes only a few hours to complete.
- Buying the right kit for your make and model is essential, as is reading and understanding the manufacturer's installation instructions.
- Superchargers and turbochargers can deliver 40 percent or greater increases in usable power.

13

Fueled
(Improving Fuel Delivery)

In This Chapter

◆ Understanding octane

◆ Fuel rails, injectors, and pumps

◆ Nitrous oxide issues

Fuel is the food that stokes that furnace under the hood we call an engine. Never take the importance of fuel for granted or dismiss it as something of little importance because without fuel, you have no power. So we're going to devote this chapter to this marvelous liquid and how to get it delivered to the engine in the most efficient manner. To get things off with an extra jolt, we'll be covering nitrous oxide, as well. And that's no laughing (gas) matter!

Causing Combustion

When the mixture of fuel and air is compressed inside the engine's cylinders and the spark from the plugs ignites it, combustion occurs. But it's not a slow-burning combustion by any means. It's a very rapid combustion that literally causes a violent explosion within the cylinder with enough power to force the piston down which, in turn, rotates the crankshaft. With all these explosions occurring in the cylinders in a predetermined order, the result is usable power that the engine delivers to the transmission. But not all fuel burns at the same rate or with the same intensity; the octane of the fuel determines these characteristics.

Octane Explained

The octane number you see at the gas pumps, 87, 91, and 93, for example, indicates how much the fuel can be compressed before it automatically ignites. Automatic ignition of the fuel, also called spontaneous ignition, is not a good thing and something you don't want to happen. Rather, you want the fuel to ignite in sync with the spark generated by the spark plugs. So why is automatic ignition something you don't want? Because compression ignition (detonation) causes knocking in your motor that will eventually lead to motor damage in most cases. The lower the octane rating of the fuel is, the greater the chance of spontaneous ignition. Conversely, the higher the octane is, the safer you are against this type of engine abuse.

The compression ratio of your motor dictates what octane you should use in your vehicle; the higher the compression ratio, the higher the octane you need to use in your ride. It's all proportional: the more compression your motor creates, the more horsepower your engine will put out. However, the down side of all this is that the higher the octane, the more expensive the price per gallon of gasoline gets.

Fuel Rails

A fuel rail is a hollow metal shaft that transports the vehicle's fuel from the chassis fuel lines to the fuel injectors which feed the engine. The fuel rail is also responsible for stabilizing the fuel pressure and flow rate to each individual injector. Additionally, the fuel rail maintains the stable position of the injectors. Keeping the injectors in a stable, fixed position is essential for maintaining the correct spray pattern of the fuel into the intake port of each cylinder.

Figure 13.1

This is a good example of an upgraded fuel system with upgraded fuel rail and upgraded injectors.

(Dave Reider photo)

Now, through our discussions you know you can perform myriad modifications to generate more horsepower. You can create more spark to better ignite the fuel, increase the engine's breathing by making the air more free flowing, or for those who really want a power boost, you have options for forced induction. The real key to reliable, consistent, and increased performance is balance—all the elements in the right proportion working in complete harmony. And this becomes more important as the mods themselves become more serious. For example, adding an air intake and/or some better sparkplug wires is not a massive overload on the motor; however, when you add a supercharger or turbocharger to your ride's engine, you'll need to compensate the extra air being fed in by adding more fuel to the mix, too.

Fuel Injectors

Think of a fuel injector as a valve that's controlled electronically by the car's computer. The computer tells the injectors to open and close, a process that repeats many times in a second. The fuel comes out a nozzle when the valve is open. This nozzle is designed to create a super-fine mist because the finer the mist, the easier the burn. The computer controls the amount of fuel the injectors release into the motor. This mist is a very precise mixture because the spark, air, and fuel must all be in the proper ratios or the motor will not function properly.

In many instances, especially when you add a supercharger or turbocharger to your vehicle, you will need to install larger fuel injectors because these larger aftermarket injectors can deliver more fuel to the motor upon each valve's opening. It is important to maintain the proper air-to-fuel ratio; if the ratio isn't correct, you can do serious damage to the engine.

Figure 13.2

Another very nice setup is shown here. It doesn't get much better than this AEM fuel rail with pressure gauge installed.

(Dave Reider photo)

Fuel injectors mount in place on the intake manifold and are held in place by the fuel rail. The fuel rail controls the amount of pressure needed to make the injectors work properly, so the injectors and the fuel rail work as a team. And it's extremely important to use the right size injectors for your particular application; if too much fuel is fed into the engine, it will flood it; if not enough fuel is delivered, the engine will sputter and possibly stall out. There is a mathematical formula for determining the right size injectors to use when you have substantially upgraded your air intake. Since this formula is fairly complex and pretty technical, it's a good idea to enlist the assistance of a professional to help you determine the correct injectors for your ride. However, once you know which injectors to use, swapping the stock units out and installing the new ones is something you can do yourself.

Fuel Pumps

In order for the fuel rails and injectors to do their jobs, the fuel must be delivered from the gas tank to these components, and that's where the fuel pump comes into play. As its name implies, it literally pumps the gas from the tank to where it's needed in the engine compartment.

Residing inside your gas tank, completely submerged, the fuel pump has a valve on one side that opens to take in fuel and pump it through the fuel line that runs underneath your car up to the fuel rail. As you can see from our discussions, each component is integral to the proper functioning of your vehicle; if you remove any one of these critical items, you won't be going anywhere, and that's a fact.

So just as we discussed the need to upgrade your injectors, you may need to upgrade your fuel pump as well. Generally, a fuel pump upgrade is for the serious performance guru or racer because you can usually upgrade your injectors one or two sizes without having to change the pump. However, if you have built a serious race machine and your car requires a lot more fuel than when it was stock, you need to upgrade the means of getting the fuel to the rail, which means upgrading the fuel pump. You can change the injectors to deliver more fuel, but if the rail isn't supplied with a sufficient amount of fuel to compensate for the additional fuel pressure needs, you're going to have a problem.

YELLOW FLAG

Changing the fuel pump can be a messy job. For starters, you want to have your tank as close to empty as possible. Secondly, and we can't stress the importance of this enough, because gasoline and its fumes are volatile and extremely flammable, proceed with extreme caution, and always have a fire extinguisher close at hand.

It's almost a 100 percent guarantee that you'll have to drop the gas tank from the vehicle to change the fuel pump. While having the car on a lift will make this job a lot easier, you can do it without a lift provided you solidly support the car with jack stands. While tank mounting varies depending on the make and model, the mounting points and/or tank support straps are generally easy to locate for removal. Once you drop the tank, removing the old pump and replacing it with the upgrade unit is a straightforward process that you can do with basic tools. It's imperative, however, that you purchase a direct-replacement upgrade unit to avoid any installation problems.

Got Juice? (Nitrous)

Dentists have used nitrous oxide, also known as "laughing gas," for over a century as a means of reducing pain and relaxing patients having dental work done. However, owing to its volatile properties, nitrous oxide has also become a popular way to extract a lot of additional power from automotive engines.

TUNER TRIVIA

Nitrous oxide, N_2O, is a colorless, almost odorless gas that English scientist and clergyman Joseph Priestley first discovered in 1793.

Nitrous—what a rush—literally! At the push of a button a nitrogen/oxygen mixture (which is what nitrous oxide is) gets released into your motor to give you extra ponies, big time. The amount of additional power is dependent on how much nitrous you allow into your motor at one time. For example, you could do a small "50" shot, or some professional race car drivers have what is called a two-stage setup for adding 500-plus horsepower worth of nitrous to their engines.

IN THE KNOW

Running "on the bottle" or "running on juice," as it is sometimes called, refers to having a nitrous oxide kit installed on your engine.

Figure 13.3

Nitrous doesn't have to be elaborate to be functional, as shown with this clean and simple bottle installation.

(Dave Reider photo)

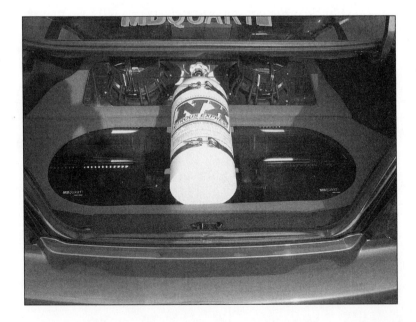

Figure 13.4

Of course, there is nothing to prevent you from going elaborate if you want to, as with this sweet twin bottle setup.

(Dave Reider photo)

The Good News and the Bad News

The good news is that this is a quick and fairly inexpensive way of adding horsepower to your motor. The down side (and by now you should realize that there always is some sort of a downside) is that it is also the most dangerous of modifications if the nitrous release is not proportioned correctly.

Figure 13.5

With this particular setup the nitrous is introduced directly into the air intake.

(Dave Reider photo)

Dry Shots

A dry shot of juice is when you spray the laughing gas (also sometimes referred to as "funny stuff") into the intake manifold where it mixes with fuel and air at the injectors. Though a bit safer on your motor, this form of use is not the most efficient or beneficial way of getting maximal power gains from nitrous oxide. The caveat with this type of installation is that you must be conservative because if you run your car too lean, the odds are you will be shopping for a replacement motor in fairly short order. Another form of a dry shot is to spray the nitrous into your intercooler. Companies, such as Nitrous Express, make kits that bolt right to the front of the intercooler for this purpose. By shooting the nitrous into the intercooler, you are making the air significantly cooler; and since colder air is more dense, the result is more air enters the intake manifold. And we've already covered the power-increasing effects of giving the engine more air to work with, remember?

Wet Shots

The other type of nitrous use is a wet injection, also known as a wet shot. While not the most common option for street machines, this method entails mixing the shot with the fuel itself. Essentially, the nitrous oxide is mixed with fuel and then fed to a fogger that sprays the combination directly into your engine's throttle body. This provides the automatic balance of air to fuel needed; however, it is not uncommon to have an excessive amount of fuel puddle up in your intake manifold, and that can create serious backfiring problems.

For the ultimate performance junkie, a direct-port wet shot is the crazy man's choice of systems. In this system each cylinder gets its own nitrous injector. A serious amount of labor is required to perform this type of installation, and you have two options. If you're lucky, you might find a prefabricated intake manifold available for your specific engine that you can just swap out. However, for the majority of installations you must have your intake manifold customized, and that will require the services of a machine shop.

Each manufacturer provides usage guidelines, tech sheets, and installation instructions with their systems. Because of the wide variety of nitrous systems available, it's impossible to give detailed installation instructions here, so our best advice is to follow the manufacturer's information explicitly.

> **YELLOW FLAG**
>
> Releasing nitrous into your engine causes the explosions within each cylinder to be significantly more violent, and that's what gives such a tremendous power boost. However, this extra violence can take its toll on the engine components if they're not up to the extra stress it will impose upon them.

Figure 13.6

Here's everything you would need to set up a killer nitrous system for your ride.

(Dave Reider photo)

How Much and for How Long

Remember, the main focus of everything that deals with engine performance modifications always comes down to one word: balance. The proper balance of air, fuel, and spark makes a better functioning motor and keeps you a happy camper. Improper balance brings with it many problems, not the least of which is ultimately a blown (as in "destroyed") motor.

Both types of nitrous systems have their good and bad points. Many people say a wet system inherently increases your fuel input, so it's better. But to counter that, it can leave fuel puddles in your intake that cause backfiring.

A dry system is not as powerful and may be less damaging; but, on the flip side, it can be very damaging if you don't have the correct combination of fuel and spark to compensate for and work with the additional oxygen.

What's more important than anything else regarding nitrous is how much you use. While each vehicle and application is different, the advice most professionals give is to start off small and work your way up. It's very important to remember that when you use a big shot, even when you do have the right fuel and spark combination, sometimes the engine itself just can't take all the extra pressure this puts on it and, ultimately, lets go. For that reason, we strongly recommend that if you use anything more than a "100" shot, you should upgrade the internal engine components to lessen the possibility of blowing up the motor.

The Least You Need to Know

◆ The more compression your engine has, the higher octane gasoline it will require.

◆ You can increase the size of your fuel injectors to deliver more fuel to the engine.

◆ The fuel pump is responsible for getting the fuel from the gas tank to the fuel rails.

◆ Nitrous oxide can add a lot of extra power to your motor, but it can only be used for short bursts.

◆ Overdoing the nitrous can cause a motor to blow-up if it is not structurally strong enough to take the additional power delivered by the funny stuff.

14

Computer Hacking (Chips and Reprogramming)

In This Chapter

- ◆ Replacement chips
- ◆ Custom programming
- ◆ Stand-alone modules

Today's engines are marvels of technology. Just a few decades ago, no computers or integrated circuits regulated anything in the vehicle, but all that has changed for the better. Thanks to the on-board computers in our vehicles, we are now able to enjoy incredible amounts of horsepower with terrific fuel economy. In addition, by *hacking* the computers a bit, we can extract even better performance. This chapter shows you how.

Getting with the Program

Some folks say there are many differences between the modern tuner and the engine builders of the hot rod and muscle car eras but, truthfully, really only one difference sets the two generations apart: our modern tuning era has the benefit of technological advancement on our side. What the old-school boys had to do manually the hard way nowadays is all done

TUNER TALK

Hacking or hacked refers to a ride that has had it's ECU programming changed, either through aftermarket chip replacement or through a downloaded program.

electronically. But that's how progress happens. And it's only natural when you stop to think about it. With all the rapid advancements in computer technology, it was inevitable and only a matter of time until auto manufacturers adapted that technology for use in vehicles.

The Engine Control Unit (ECU) is a small computer that monitors all engine sensors and controls all engine functions for fuel delivery, ignition timing, rev limiter, speed limiter, valve timing control, and emission systems. This computer operates based on a set of values the manufacturer created. These values, generally considered conservative, although somewhat restricted, leave a lot to be desired by the performance enthusiast. And that's where the modern game began. The manufacturers use restrictive programming to keep emissions well within EPA guidelines, to keep fuel economy figures high and to increase engine life.

Chip Replacement

There are a couple of ways to get more performance out of the ECU, and the simpler upgrade consists of removing the stock program chip and installing a new reprogrammed chip that has remapped control parameters to maximize engine performance.

In many instances, people may only upgrade the chip because just changing to a reprogrammed chip allows you to tweak your fuel economy and stretch your gas mileage, sometimes quite significantly. However, for those vehicles that have had air, fuel, and ignition upgrades installed, the computer needs to be reprogrammed to maximize the functionality of these upgrades.

Even though you've made the aftermarket parts exchanges, the computer sensors (which are all throughout the engine) are still "seeing" the original parts; the computer needs a wake-up call to let it know about the upgraded parts, so it can instruct the motor how to function with them advantageously.

Chip replacement is a do-it-yourself project that will take only about an hour or less in most cases and is really not hard to perform.

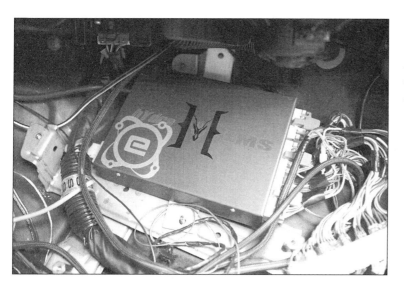

Figure 14.1

This rectangular box is actually a high-tech replacement computer installed in a Subaru WRX.

(Dave Reider photo)

Most factory computers (ECUs) are located on the front passenger side of the car, usually installed in the kick panel or under the carpet where the bottom of the dashboard meets the carpet. Carefully remove the kick panel and pull back the carpet to expose the computer which will be easy to identify because dozens of wires run into it. From this point, simply follow the step-by-step instructions provided with your new replacement chip, and then just reverse the order you took things apart to put everything back together. It's really that simple. Be sure, however, to observe the chip manufacturer's precautions about handling the chip, working with static electricity concerns, and not bending the "legs" of the chip.

Reprogramming with a Laptop/Notebook

Some of the newer cars don't come with a replaceable chip but have the computer itself as an inclusive unit. In many instances, you can send out your whole unit to have it reprogrammed, though this does put your vehicle out of service for a while.

You do have a couple of other alternatives, however. Companies, such as Hypertech, sell a small hand-held device that you connect to the vehicle's factory computer and use to upload a tweaked program to it. Although this is a great aftermarket improvement over the stock programming, the down side is that it's usually a "one program fits all" standard upgrade.

There is also the ability to program your car's computer via laptop-uploadable programs. These are usually obtained from professional vehicle tuners who map out each individual curve on a cell-by-cell line basis for your particular car. Fine-tuning a custom car can potentially take days and many tries to get it just right. But the best part of our technology is that you can fine-tune a car from the passenger's seat and never have to get dirty in the engine bay as they did "in the old days."

Figure 14.2

Spaghetti, anyone? Because virtually every system in the car is connected to the computer, plenty of wires come from all over the place and go into the ECU.

(Dave Reider photo)

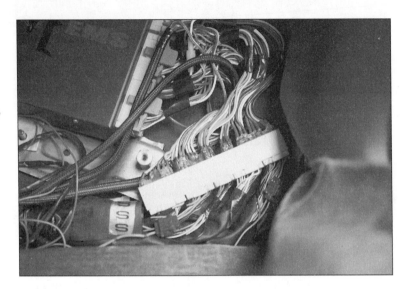

Stand-Alone Modules

In some instances, you may have to use a stand-alone computer and completely custom wire all the necessary sensors and modules. This is often the case with the serious track car or when someone has done a complete *engine swap*. When you completely change to an engine not offered as a factory option, your computer and factory wiring harness will not match this different engine's needs. Sometimes you can get lucky, as some companies, such as Painless Wiring, make complete vehicle wiring harnesses. Other times you will have to hard wire everything yourself.

> **TUNER TALK**
>
> **Engine swapping** is replacing the factory motor with an entirely different engine that is not an exact OEM replacement unit.

The Least You Need to Know

♦ You can either replace or reprogram the control chips in your car's ECU.

♦ If other modifications have been made to the engine, their performance gains can only be fully realized when the computer is aware of the new components.

♦ You can tune the ECU via the passenger seat rather than in the engine bay.

♦ An engine swap will necessitate changing the computer and wiring harness to match the new motor.

Chapter 15

Power Exhaling (Hi-Flow Exhaust)

In This Chapter

- ◆ Lowering exhaust restriction
- ◆ Hi-perf headers
- ◆ Catalytic converters
- ◆ Cat-back replacement

You've learned about getting more air and fuel into the engine, increasing the spark for bigger and better combustion, and even using nitrous for an extra boost. So it stands to reason with all this extra power being generated that more exhaust gases are produced. Just as increasing the engine's "inhaling" will increase power, helping it to "exhale" easier will add some extra ponies, too. And that's the focus of what we talk about in this chapter.

Blowing It Out

In keeping with our overall philosophy of "balance" when it comes to making performance upgrades, we must keep one more key component in equal harmony, and that is the exhaust system.

The job of the muffler is to quiet the sounds the engine produces in operation. And now that your engine is producing more combustion, you have to improve the way it releases the exhaust gases. The interior of a muffler is designed to act as a sound barrier to minimize the amount of audible sound produced by the engine. The problem for performance people is this: the quieter the muffler, the more restrictive the exhaust system is. Restrictive exhausts not only restrict the noise, but they also restrict power, too. Upgrading the exhaust system will allow the engine to exhale better and breathe more freely. But as with all the other mods, you don't want to overdo this, either. If the exhaust is too nonrestrictive, the force, known as back pressure, won't be sufficient and will disrupt that perfect balance that you are seeking to achieve for optimal performance.

Low-Restriction Muffler Upgrades

The easiest and most cost effective exhaust upgrade is installing a low-restriction muffler. Dozens of companies, such as Flowmaster, Borla, Magnaflow, and Apexi, make enhanced-flow mufflers that will let your ride exhale easier and better. These mufflers are less restrictive internally and allow expelling exhaust gases an easier route of release. Muffler upgrades will also enhance your vehicle's overall performance. While upgrading the muffler by itself probably won't make a difference you can feel, combined with the other modifications we have talked about, improving things a little here and a little there can easily make your engine produce a significant amount of additional horsepower that you will definitely feel when you step on the *loud pedal*.

> **TUNER TALK**
>
> **Loud pedal** is a slang expression for the accelerator pedal. It probably came into use by virtue of the fact that an engine produces more audible sound under hard acceleration than when idling.

Figure 15.1

This is a typical example of an aftermarket replacement muffler.

(Dave Reider photo)

Low-restriction mufflers come in two forms: direct replacement and universal fit. The direct replacement units are exactly the same size as the original stock mufflers and install without problems or requiring any special modifications.

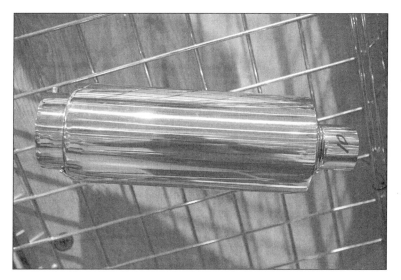

Figure 15.2

Here we see a polished replacement "universal-fit" performance muffler.

(Dave Reider photo)

If you choose to go the universal route, however, make sure you know what the clearances are under your car so you get the right replacement piece. Although several clamp-on muffler options are out there, it's always best to ensure the proper seal by having a professional weld the new unit in place once you're satisfied with the fit.

Figure 15.3

This is not your typical-looking aftermarket replacement performance muffler, for sure.

(Dave Reider photo)

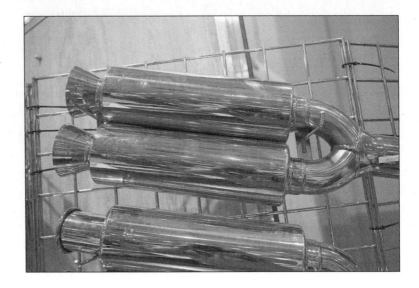

Headers

Headers are one of the easiest bolt-on accessories you can install to significantly improve an engine's performance. The goal of upgrading to headers is to make it easier for the engine to exhale and release the spent exhaust from the cylinders.

When upgrading your ride to headers, you increase the overall diameter of the exhaust piping. Each cylinder has its own exhaust pipe, and each one is the exact same length; they all meet together at what we refer to as the collector. Each pipe is the same exact length so that the exhaust gasses arrive equally in the collector and eliminate the chance of back pressure by the cylinders sharing the collector.

Companies, such as Kooks and DC Sport, make direct bolt-on replacement headers. Though the process of swapping your standard exhaust manifold out for headers is fairly simple, be forewarned that you may first have to remove many engine components that impede the installation path of the headers. However, if you follow the orderly process of unbolting, labeling, and rebolting things after you install the headers, the task is fairly easy and shouldn't require any special tools to accomplish.

Just changing the wheels and tires on your ride can make a huge difference in how it looks. Here's a Cadillac STS with the factory stock wheels and tires on it.

(Tom Benford photo)

Here's the same STS outfitted with Zinik Z5 Ikeda 20" chrome wheels and Pirelli Pzero Nero tires from The Tire Rack on it. 245/30s are on front with 255/30s on the rear.

(Tom Benford photo)

*TG Designs' wide body Scion TC was seen on bill-
boards all across America.*

(Dave Reider photo)

*Tommy Tran was one of the first builders to use a
Mercedes as his canvas and what a creation it is.*

(Dave Reider photo)

*The slammed stance on this VW is extremely
aggressive.*

(Dave Reider photo)

*Robert Weinert teamed up with DuPont
to create this one-of-a-kind Acura TL.*

(Dave Reider photo)

Albert Fung and his Toyota Celica know how to get attention at any event they attend.

(Dave Reider photo)

This S2000 is sporting a set of sweet Veilside hard-to-find wheels.

(Dave Reider photo)

Scott Schenfield used tons of chrome and carbon Kevlar accessories to really make his one-of-a-kind Viper stand out. But this baby isn't just about looks—she's got the power to match it.

(Dave Reider photo)

One might think this builder has a thing for mermaids.

(Dave Reider photo)

Tajai Das and his Acura Integra took NCCA top honors in the 2005 Show Circuit.
This car, known as the Acurabot, is a true piece of automotive art.

(Dave Reider photo)

This Nissan 180SX is all ready for some sliding action.

(Dave Reider photo)

Certainly not your average station wagon with its huge chrome wheels and wild marble green paint job, this Honda Accord can't be missed.

(Dave Reider photo)

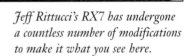

Jeff Rittucci's RX7 has undergone a countless number of modifications to make it what you see here.

(Dave Reider photo)

This bright orange Scion XB knows how to wow the crowd, alright.

(Dave Reider photo)

The orange and green paint combination definitely stands out big-time.

(Dave Reider photo)

The intricate skull graphics on this Acura Integra make you wonder what this car's owner does for a living.

(Dave Reider photo)

Thanks to an airbag suspension this Scion XA sits slammed when showing off.

(Dave Reider photo)

This Ford Mustang owned by Jillian Morton is a fine example that modern tuning has no gender restraints.

(Dave Reider photo)

This wide body Chevy Aveo exemplifies how compact cars can be highly modified, too.

(Dave Reider photo)

The color coordination of the body and wheels on this Honda Del Sol makes it stand out in a crowd.

(Dave Reider photo)

This Gold Mitsubishi Eclipse was fitted with a set of R34 Skyline headlights where the stock ones used to be.

(Dave Reider photo)

This Honda engine sports a pair of gold anodized upgrade cam gears.

(Dave Reider photo)

Is this the cockpit of a 747 or Scion XB? We sure had to think twice!

(Dave Reider photo)

A Chevrolet Corvette always makes a great canvas to start with. Hosting wild graphics and an intricate audio/video system, this is one 'Vette you don't want to mess with.

(Dave Reider photo)

The color-matched body and fiber glassed subwoofer enclosure make a statement in this Honda Civic.

(Dave Reider photo)

Figure 15.4

These polished headers are screaming "look at me" when the hood is up. They not only look good, but they also provide a real performance boost.

(Dave Reider photo)

Hi-Flow Catalytic Converters

The catalytic converter, in simple terms, is an exhaust filter in the path between the headers or exhaust manifold and the muffler. The EPA's emission standards mandate the use of catalytic converters as the best solution to reduce the atmospheric pollutants your engine produces.

While that's all well and good, in truth, the catalytic converter in its factory form is one of the most restrictive pieces and is largely responsible for holding back your car's performance. Several companies make hi-flow catalytic converter replacements that will allow your car to breath better, which, in turn, increases performance while still allowing you to remain environmentally responsible and keeping your ride legal.

> ## YELLOW FLAG
>
> Never eliminate the catalytic converter on your ride, as this is a super big no-no if you want to keep your ride street legal. Without a doubt, you're going to hear about people who get rid of their cat converter and connect a straight pipe in its place, saying "forget it—I don't need it." While some people actually do this, we can guarantee these cars will fail their state's motor vehicle inspection. And to make matters worse, if they get caught without a cat converter on their car, the fines can be very costly. In fact, the car may even be impounded! Stay environmentally green, and go with a high flow replacement unit; it's the responsible (and smart) thing to do.

Cat-Back Exhaust Systems

While more costly than a muffler replacement, many enthusiasts opt for a cat-back system. This means they replace everything after (or in back of) the catalytic converter. The benefit of this as opposed to just a muffler exchange is that all the plumbing (pipe work) between the catalytic converter and the muffler gets replaced. So, if you go with hi-flow cat and an upgraded muffler without changing the connecting pipes, you're really short-changing yourself as far as performance goes. Of course, you will see a significant performance improvement, but performance will be much greater if you replace the stock plumbing with pipes that are larger in diameter because they'll permit more exhaust fumes to travel at the same time than stock pipes.

All the earlier mentioned companies and others offer an array of cat-back replacement systems for most car makes and models. The really nice thing about replacement systems like these is that they use all of the stock factory mounting points, making the installation a true unbolt and rebolt process with a direct-fit exchange. The hardest part of an installation like this is the labor it will take to free-up those stubborn bolts holding your factory system in place. Better eat your Wheaties first!

> ## YELLOW FLAG
>
> Before you begin, make sure your car is cold and has been sitting for several hours. Exhaust components get extremely hot, and you don't want to get burned when working.

Installing Exhaust Systems

Anytime you have to work on the underside of your ride, having a lift at your disposal makes life infinitely easier. Having said this, few of us have a lift, so the best alternative is to elevate the vehicle and support it with sturdy jack stands. If you decide to install your own upgrade exhaust components, we advise you to make every effort to purchase direct-replacement parts; they will make your installation a lot smoother and faster.

You will need a reasonably large amount of ground clearance to work effectively under the car, so get the vehicle as high as your jack and stands will allow. Next, locate all the mounting points for the hangers because you'll have to release these connections that secure the system to the frame. Spraying any bolts you need to remove with a bit of lubricant like WD-40 will help make breaking them free easier.

Figure 15.5

When the going gets rough doing an exhaust installation, reach for the WD-40 spray. This stuff works wonders at freeing up the stubborn nuts and bolts you may encounter when removing the stock exhaust components.

(Tom Benford photo)

Now disconnect the pipe attached to the cat converter, and your stock system should drop free. Assemble the new system pieces before getting back underneath the car. Align the new system so the mounting points line up properly; connect your new pipe to the cat converter; and then mount your muffler to the appropriate hanger.

Lastly, connect the remaining hangers that go between the muffler and the cat. While virtually all of these aftermarket systems are bolt-on units, we recommend you have the connection points welded to ensure you have no exhaust fume leaks coming from your system. Few things are worse or more annoying than hearing a whistle coming from a leaky connection every time you accelerate.

The Least You Need to Know

- ◆ Not removing any restrictions in the exhaust system will reduce the performance gain potential of other mods you have made.

- ◆ Headers are an easy bolt-on modification that will significantly improve performance.

- ◆ Catalytic converters are required by law, and you can get a severe fine by running your car on the street without one.

- ◆ A shot of WD-40 or other good spray lubricant makes removing stubborn exhaust system nuts and bolts easier.

Part 5

Hit the Road

Okay, we're impressed with all the performance mods you made under the hood. Your ride is really a performance machine now that deserves and commands respect wherever you take it. But you're not done yet—not by a long shot.

Having all this power at your disposal doesn't do too much good if you can't deliver it effectively where it counts—to the pavement! While your stock suspension components, wheels, and tires were just fine for your stock motor, what you've got under the hood is putting out a lot more now than when it left the factory. So you're going to have to beef up the under-carriage assemblies to handle all the extra horses.

We're talking springs and shocks, strut and sway bars, better brakes, and trick wheels and tires here—after all, it wouldn't be a truly righteous ride if we didn't go the full boat, now would it? So get on board and let's take it to the next level.

16

Shocks, Springs, and Coilovers

In This Chapter

◆ The role of the suspension

◆ Upgrading suspension components

◆ Alternative suspensions

Without suspension, your vehicle would have a bone-jarring ride that would transmit every crack, pothole, and other irregularity in the roadway surface through the chassis and into your body. And, if that isn't enough, your tires would hop and skip erratically every time you encountered one of these roadway anomalies, causing you to lose traction and expose yourself to innumerable dangers. So, as you see, the suspension has some important jobs and deserves your full attention here.

Smoothing Out Bumps and Getting a Grip

When customizing a car for performance, the first thing to get attention is the engine in an attempt to get more horsepower out of it. The truth of the matter is that the more horsepower your engine produces, the greater the stress that is put on the rest of the car's mechanical parts. The question that you have to ask yourself is this: what good is more horsepower if it can't be delivered to the road? This is just another example of achieving overall balance; as you improve your power output, you must also improve the car's grip to the pavement.

You can improve your suspension in several different ways, based on the style of driving you prefer. If you like to go straight and fast, use different components than someone who likes to handle fast, sharp turns. So the first question you need to ask yourself is what type of a driver are you?

What Your Suspension Does

Simply put, your suspension's job is to take most of the road abuse your vehicle encounters so you can enjoy the drive. Your suspension is made of several components that work together to absorb roadway imperfections. To better understand, it might help to compare your suspension to a pair of sneakers. A nice new pair of sneakers has a thick cushioned sole, which every time you step down absorbs the pressure your foot makes on impact, giving you an easy walk so comfortable it feels like you're gliding. On the other hand, think of when you're out washing the car in your two-year-old junk sneakers; because the sneakers are worn out and uncomfortable, you feel every little thing when you step down. Now, think of your suspension in the same way; the only difference is that your sneakers are supporting a couple of hundred pounds while your car's suspension is supporting two or three thousand pounds.

Your suspension absorbs all the impact your wheels make; a worn-out suspension will give you a very uncomfortable ride and you'll bounce around like a bobble head. A new luxury car has soft suspension that tries to absorb everything so you can have the smoothest ride possible, whereas a high-performance sport car like a Corvette C6 has stiffer suspension that provides better handling. Improving your suspension components can help you control your car better whether you're on a track and need a stiff suspension or you're cruising and want that soft luxury feel. The good news is that you can customize your suspension to fit your personal taste.

Figure 16.1

Here is the stock ride height of a Scion TC. Notice the amount of space between the top of the tire and the edge of the wheel well.

(Dave Reider photo)

Figure 16.2

Now compare how much less tire-to-fender well space there is on this Scion TC with coilover lowering shocks installed.

(Dave Reider photo)

Upgrading Shocks and Springs

One of the first modifications usually made to the suspension is to replace the stock units with lowering springs. Lowering springs, made by companies such as Eibach, remove the excessive wheel well gap between the tires and fenders to give the ride a sleeker, more aggressive stance. Aside from the aesthetic benefits of lowering springs, they are quite functional, too. By lowering the center of gravity and having the car sit lower to the ground, you will experience a noticeable improvement when taking turns as the car will "roll" less.

You almost always have to remove the shocks and struts in order to install replacement springs, so this is an ideal time to upgrade these components as well. Think about it: you're already going to do all of the labor to replace the springs; the only additional costs for upgrading the shocks and struts at this point are for the new parts. Performing a shock and strut change with high-performance versions from such companies as Tokico will make your car ride smoother and handle better.

Figure 16.3

A brand new K Sport coilover is looking for a new ride to call home—maybe yours!

(Dave Reider photo)

Upgrading to a better gas shock will assist in controlling the action of the springs because the job of the shocks is to compress and extend with the springs when encountering roadway imperfections. The faster the suspension moves, the more resistance the shock creates, and it self-adjusts to road conditions. The shocks help to absorb some of the road impacts (or shocks, hence the name *shock absorber*) your car encounters while in motion.

Adjustable Combinations

Those who want to get the most out of their car's shock and strut combination should look into an adjustable coilover package. Companies like Tein, JIC, D2, and dozens of others make packages that range from 5- up to 36-way adjustables. With these packages you can adjust how stiff or soft you want the ride to be and, on some, you can even adjust the *camber* to "*tuck*" your wheels.

TUNER TALK

Camber refers to a wheel's inward or outward tilt from the vertical and is measured in degrees. A negative camber is present when the wheels are closer at the top than at the bottom when viewed from either the front or the rear; conversely, positive camber is present when the wheels are further apart at the top than at the bottom when viewed the same way.

Tucking is to make the wheel well sit so low over the tire and rim that the top edge of the rim is almost hidden.

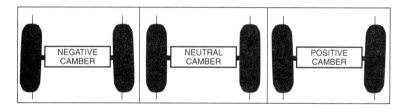

Figure 16.4

Here's an illustration of negative, neutral, and positive camber.

(Tom Benford illustration)

Adjustable shocks are ideal since they give you the best of all worlds. You can set them to be very stiff when it's time to hit the road course, or set them to be soft and cushy when you're out on the town cruising the venue. The nicest thing about them is that you can change the settings with a simple adjustment in your driveway that takes only a few seconds at each wheel with the provided tool.

Figure 16.5

Here's an adjustable coilover. Easy and quick to adjust, these shocks allow you to custom tailor the ride stiffness to suit your particular needs and preferences.

(Dave Reider photo)

Alternative Suspensions

Although high-performance shock and spring combination replacements are the most common mods done, we must mention two additional types of suspensions: air suspensions and hydraulic suspensions. While both of these suspension systems are more for show than for functionality, they've both developed their own culture segments.

Air Suspension Systems

Air suspensions are similar to spring and shock combinations in that both systems consist of cylinders that sit between the wheel and the body of a car. However, air suspensions use air to function rather than the compressed gas inside a gas shock. The compressive qualities of air absorb the road vibrations.

TUNER TALK

Slammed refers to a vehicle that has been lowered as much as possible while still being drivable.

In truth, however, modern customizing builders don't install air suspensions because they make the ride smoother; actually, most air kits will make the ride considerably rougher. The beauty of an air suspension is that when you are chilling at your local spot or at a car show, the air suspension can be totally deflated so the car actually sits on the ground for that ultra-*slammed* look. Essentially, customizers choose air suspensions because of the aggressive stance they can give the car when parked, not for their functionality on the road.

Hydraulic Suspensions

When you think "low rider," you probably think "hydraulics," right? But it's highly inaccurate to say that all low riders utilize hydraulics because, in fact, they don't. There is an entire segment of auto enthusiasts other than low riders who are really into hydraulic suspensions.

Hydraulic suspensions, also called "hydros" for short, use an array of cylinders and pumps controlled by a switch box located in the interior of the car. You can use these pumps to perform all kinds of functions. With hydraulics, you can lift one corner, one side, or everything at the same time. In addition to cars, hydraulic suspensions are very popular with the sport truck crowd.

Although hydraulics can be fun to play with and have lots of "wow" crowd appeal, they produce the stiffest ride imaginable, so they're really not the way to go if you plan to enjoy cruising in your ride. However, an entire community of enthusiasts build their cars completely around their hydraulic suspensions. Whatever turns you on, right?

> **IN THE KNOW**
>
> A phenomenon known as "wheel hop" occurs when a wheel leaves the ground while in motion, usually under hard acceleration or when encountering a roadway irregularity. Suspension that is too stiff can also promote wheel hop, which is not desirable.

The Least You Need to Know

- Suspension modifications are necessary to keep the balance when engine horsepower has been increased.

- Having extra power available does no good if you can't deliver it to the road surface efficiently.

- When upgrading your springs, it makes sense to upgrade your shocks and struts at the same time because these items are already going to be removed from the vehicle.

- Air and hydraulic suspension systems look cool but are not practical for actual cruising.

17

Strut Bars, Sway Bars, and More

In This Chapter

◆ Other important suspension parts

◆ Making the right choices

◆ Control and trailing arms

As you've already learned, suspension is a critical component of your vehicle. Without it, not only would your ride be uncomfortable, but the vehicle also would not handle properly either. However, there's more to the total suspension picture than just springs and shocks, and that's what we're going to delve into here. So open up your eyes, and see the total suspension picture as we unveil it.

Serving Their Purpose

Although springs and shocks/struts are the main components that make up your vehicle's suspension, other parts are crucial to performance machines as well. Even though they may seem very simplistic, until you understand what they do, they can be a little confusing. So here's the fast track on what your suspension is all about.

Strut bars connect on the top shock tower housing and run across the car from the driver's side to the passenger side. Sway bars connect in a similar fashion, although they attach on the underside of the car. Other critical suspension parts include bushings (rubber or polyurethane grommets that separate and cushion the suspension parts), control arms, and trailing arms that help prevent wheel hop and keep those tires touching the pavement. So, as you see, there's a lot more to suspension than you probably thought.

Figure 17.1

This is a nice example of a polished strut bar. Notice that it connects both shock towers by traversing the engine.

(Andy Goodman photo)

Strut bars and sway bars help control the roll you feel when your car goes into a turn. Both of these bars act as weight transfer devices that move the gravitational force from one side of the body to the other. They do this by keeping the shock/strut towers moving in exact harmony. Without them, the shock towers would move independently from each other because there's no connection between them and they move based on whatever imperfections they encounter on the road. Since the strut bars bolt across the top of the shock towers, they result in producing suspension components that become tighter and much more in sync with each other.

If your car isn't equipped with sway bars from the factory (although most newer cars are), your car will have a noticeable amount of body roll. As with everything else, however, balance is the key. If you overcompensate with a sway bar that's too aggressive, you will hinder the side-by-side independence of your suspension. By helping to stabilize the exact locations of the shock towers, especially upon road impacts, they actually help to keep your car on the ground better to gain more traction and control when driving, especially when going into a turn.

In the movie *The Fast and The Furious,* there are over 15,000 individual sound effects in the first street race!

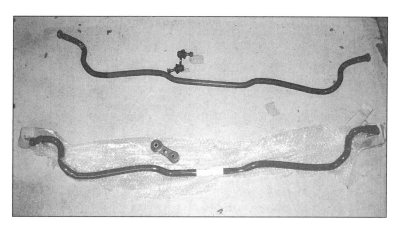

Figure 17.2

Shown here is a stock sway bar at the top and an aftermarket replacement below it. Notice how the upgrade aftermarket piece is much thicker in diameter.

(Andy Goodman photo)

Choosing What's Best for You

Before running out and buying a bunch of aftermarket suspension products, you first need to determine what type of driver you are. Here are a few questions to help you make that determination.

◆ Do you punch it when there's open road ahead, or do you like to take the highway off-ramps at excessive speeds?

◆ Do you prefer drag racing or touring?

◆ Do you prefer a stiff ride or a smooth ride?

Regardless of which type of driver you are, the "one custom mod that fits all" change is to upgrade the springs.

Taking it to the next level, if you prefer the go-fast-quick performance, the next upgrade to consider is the shocks. You'll probably want to get a set of performance shocks that are rated based on the vehicle's weight distribution when accelerating off of the line.

Kicking it up a notch further, you'll do well to stiffen up the rear sway bar so when you step on it and the weight transfers the pressure from the front to the rear, the distribution of force will be evenly distributed through the sides of the car. And if you're really a hardcore performance guru, you may want to upgrade the control arms, too.

If you are more concerned with a luxury-smooth ride and soft turning, then check out the high-quality electronically-controlled suspension systems available. With these you can set the ride comfort by controlling the stiffness of the shock spring combinations through a control panel that mounts inside the cockpit.

Figure 17.3

Here you can see an after-market sway bar installation. Notice how it goes across the whole width of the car from one side to the other.

(Andy Goodman photo)

You can also consider a front strut bar that helps to keep the shock towers in sync with each other.

And for the driver who wants it all, go with a set of fully adjustable coilovers that let you set them to be stiff for great performance response or loose for daily driving. The choices are all yours.

TUNER TRIVIA

In the movie *2 Fast and 2 Furious,* the Saleen Mustang that crashes in the highway scene is not an actual Saleen Mustang. It is a V6 Mustang modified with a Saleen body kit.

Decisions: Top, Bottom, Front, and Rear

Understandably, with so many suspension options available, the decision becomes rather difficult to make. If you have the ability and the green to revamp your entire suspension in one shot, by all means, go for it. Doing everything all at the same time will definitely cost you less for labor in the long run because everything gets disassembled and reassembled only once.

Many builders, for one reason or another, do their suspensions piece-by-piece, slowly but surely installing all the right components one at a time. Most start with springs, shocks, and struts, then install strut and sway bars.

There are two routes you can take here. If you're concerned with performance, start with the top front engine strut bar, then the bottom rear bar, and follow with the top rear bar.

Many of today's high-performance machines come equipped with sway bars, so upgrading them simply means removing and replacing the stock bars with thicker diameter units.

If you're primarily concerned with style and appearance, go with a polished or chromed front strut bar, then the rear strut bar. The appearance of underside sway bars should be of little concern because they won't be seen.

Control and Trailing Arms

Going well beyond the basic suspension mods, those who want the ultimate suspension improvements will look into upgrading their vehicle's control arms and trailing arms. These components help stabilize wheel hop and literally keep the rubber on the road. They attach to the chassis and manage the movement of the wheels so that it is in sync with the body of the car.

Figure 17.4

Here's a Subaru WRX sporting a complete aftermarket suspension setup: new control arms, stabilizer bars, and sway bar. This car must handle like butter.

(Andy Goodman photo)

Control arms are critical to your vehicle; if they did not exist, your car would be all over the road. Upgrading these components will help your suspension move in a tighter, more cohesive pattern.

Trailing arms are seen in some specific types of suspension like the older Volkswagens, but they aren't very popular in today's vehicles due to the amount of space they take up. But if you have an older machine that you want to modernize for better performance, you should definitely consider upgrading the trailing arms, too.

The Least You Need to Know

◆ The suspension system involves a lot of parts in addition to springs and shocks.

◆ Strut bars connect the shock towers and keep them in sync with each other.

◆ Electronically-controlled suspension systems permit you to dial-in the ride you want from inside the cockpit.

◆ Upgrading the control arms and (if applicable) the trailing arms will increase the efficiency of the suspension and the handling of the vehicle.

Chapter **18**

Better Binders for Improved Stopping

In This Chapter

- ◆ The pressure, friction, and heat relationship
- ◆ The enemy, heat
- ◆ Upgrades—mild to extreme

Here's a statement you can regard as gospel truth: go-fast cars need stop-fast brakes. All too often the majority of attention is spent on making the engine produce more horsepower and getting it to the ground. Improving the braking power is often only an afterthought, and this is really a bad thing. As we've stressed throughout this book, balance in all of your ride's components and systems is crucial to achieve the best all-around performance. When it comes to brakes, we can't stress the importance of this balance enough. That's why we're devoting this entire chapter to brakes as if your life depends upon them; in truth, it does!

More "Whoa" Power

Brakes are another crucial part to building a complete custom ride. Often overlooked by many builders, brakes are one of the most recognizable performance upgrades you can make to your ride. Big brake upgrades can be readily seen at anytime. More important than just good looks is their functionality. By virtue of the mods you've probably done by now, your car is generating more power so it's capable of faster off-the-line starts and maintaining higher speeds. With all this additional power and your suspension upgrades, it only stands to reason that you should have extra stopping ability for your new performance machine, right?

Figure 18.1

These are the main components of a modern automotive disc brake: 1) disc, 2) caliper and pads, and 3) wheel lugs.

(Tom Benford illustration)

Performance Pads

Brake pads are the components inside the *caliper* that actually create friction by rubbing against the rotor. The more you step on the brake pedal, the more pressure the caliper creates by pushing the pad harder against the rotor to make the vehicle stop. Standard semi-metallic pads are the basic, standard pads that come on the car from the factory. Companies such as Hawk Performance make high performance pads specifically designed to deliver smoother and better-stopping ability.

> **TUNER TALK**
>
> In a disc brake, the **caliper** is a housing for the cylinder, pistons, and brake pads, connected to the hydraulic system. The caliper holds the brake pads so they straddle the brake disc.

In addition to better stopping power, upgraded performance pads also are known to give off much less brake dust residue than their OEM counterparts, and this is a good thing when it comes to keeping your wheels nice and clean. Eventually, all brake pads are "must replace" parts, so the next time your car is due for a pad change, why not upgrade to a better performance-compound pad that will enhance your braking ability? They only cost a little more than stock replacement pads, but they deliver a lot more stopping power.

Hi-Tech Rotors

Approximately every 30,000 to 40,000 miles your brake pads come due for replacing, so why not consider upgrading your *rotors* at this time as well?

TUNER TALK

In a disc brake, the **rotor** is the actual rotating steel disc (hence the name "disc brake") that the brake pads press against to stop the vehicle.

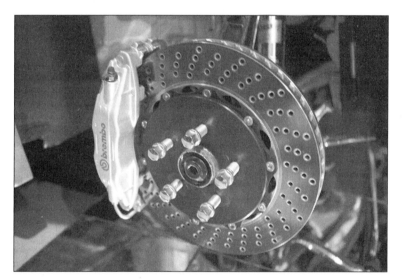

Figure 18.2

Shown here is a great example of a cross-drilled rotor. All the holes are vents that disperse heat better to prevent rotor warping.

(Dave Reider photo)

Friction is the force that brings your car to a stop. This friction is created by the caliper pressing the brake pad into the rotor, and the more pressure that is applied, the more friction is created. But along with friction comes the rotor's worst enemy: heat. Heat is a natural byproduct of friction, and the more friction created, the more heat generated. Both the pad and the rotor have to endure this abuse every time you come to a stop. The more heat increases, the less stopping power the brakes have, so it's highly desirable to prevent brake heat buildup as much as possible.

Figure 18.3

Compare this stock brake setup on a Scion TC to ...

(Dave Reider photo)

Figure 18.4

... this big brake kit on a Scion TC. Notice the much more aggressive look.

(Dave Reider photo)

Companies such as Powerstop, Stainless Steel Brakes, Wilwood, Precision Brakes, and others make vented rotors such as cross-drilled, slotted, or both that allow the rotor to breathe better and help disburse the heat. Powerstop claims their rotors run about two hundred degrees cooler than stock rotors, and that's quite a temperature difference.

Have you ever experienced a shimmy when you are driving that only occurs when you apply the brakes? And the more you apply the brakes, the worse it gets? The cause is most likely due to warped rotors. This occurs because excessive heat actually warps the metal that the rotor is made of. By upgrading to cross-drilled and/or slotted rotors, you'll have better braking ability, and you'll also lengthen the intervals between pad and rotor changes since the heat that wears on both will be dramatically reduced.

Big Brake Kits

Serious performance aficionados should consider a big brake upgrade kit. While going this route is considerably more expensive than just doing a pad and rotor upgrade, a big brake kit will totally replace your OEM braking system with higher performance components all the way around.

Figure 18.5

These Wilwood brakes fill the entire area behind the wheel; if they were any bigger, there would definitely be clearance issues, something to be careful of when upgrading to a big brake kit.

Bolt-on kits can be as simple as a brake pad and rotor upgrade or as extensive as complete systems featuring all new calipers, upgraded rotors, hubs, mounting hats, brake pads, and all the associated hardware.

Companies such as Brembo, Wilwood, and endless others offer complete bolt-on kits that you can install in your driveway with a basic tool set. These kits will give you an extra safety margin and also give your car a much more aggressive look. What's not to love here?

YELLOW FLAG

When upgrading to a big brake kit, make sure the new rotor will clear the inner diameter of your wheel. For example, if you're running 16" wheels, odds are that a 15" big brake upgrade kit won't work due to lack of clearance.

Multi-Piston Calipers

The caliper is the brake component that actually applies the pressure that squeezes the pads against the rotor. A piston housed inside the caliper does this job. Most cars come with single-piston calipers; this means that in one spot the pressure is greatest (right where the piston itself is located) and the further away the pad is from that area, the less effectively the pressure is applied.

Since braking is essentially all about force to generate friction, it stands to reason that a multiple-piston caliper will have multiple pressure points to distribute that friction more evenly along the entire surface of the brake pad, resulting in more efficient braking force. Pressure is the key to successful stopping, so the more pressure that you can apply, the quicker the vehicle will stop.

Most upgraded aftermarket big brake kits usually come with at least -piston calipers, but multi-piston calipers are usually available as an optional upgrade. Extreme builders of 1,000hp machines have been known to utilize 15" rotors with multi-piston calipers, but this is really over the top.

Besides the performance aspect of upgraded brakes, they are also very visible through most aftermarket rims. Because of this, it is very common to have the upgraded calipers *powder coated* to accent the entire vehicle and give the brakes a custom one-off touch for extra eye appeal.

> **TUNER TALK**
>
> **Powder coating** is a dry coating method in which fine clear or pigmented powder particles, containing resin, modifiers, and possibly a curing agent, are electrostatically sprayed onto a substrate and heated (melted) in an oven to form a continuous film. Powder coating is much more durable than paint and generally impervious to high temperatures, making it ideal for use on many automotive components.

Better Brake Lines

The brake lines are the conduit through which the brake fluid necessary to make your brakes function flows. When you upgrade to bigger rotors and higher piston calipers, the brake system is able to work harder and more efficiently by creating more pressure. But since the entire brake system is based on pressure, it's critical that the brake lines are capable of handling these increased pressure demands.

While it usually isn't necessary to change your brake lines if you've only upgraded the pads and rotors, if you upgrade to multi-piston calipers you should consider upgrading the brake lines as well to make sure the balance (there's that magic word again!) is maintained.

If you choose to go the big brake kit route, the recommended lines for the upgrade will be included in a stainless steel braided version with your kit purchase. These stainless steel lines are not only functional, but they look good, too.

The Least You Need to Know

- The need to be able to stop quickly increases as the car's power and speed increases.

- Excessive heat can cause brake rotors to warp.

- Upgraded brakes are functional and look good, too.

- When you upgrade to multi-piston calipers, upgrade the brake lines as well.

Chapter **19**

Tires and Wheels

In This Chapter

- ◆ Types of tires
- ◆ The world of wheels
- ◆ Going bigger

It's time to take stock—rolling stock, that is. We've improved engine performance, suspension, and braking, so it's time to turn our attention to the wheels and tires; after all, that's really where the rubber meets the road, isn't it? Now that you know what we're talking about in this chapter, let's get rolling!

Round and Round We Go

Most folks don't have a clue what all the writing on the sidewall of a tire means; it just seems like a bunch of mumbo-jumbo. But rest assured that each and every letter and number on the sidewall has an extremely important meaning that tells you exactly what the tire is all about. They also serve a purpose for mechanics, too, by telling them what type of tire to use in an OEM replacement situation.

But if you're building a custom machine, the rubber you choose will have a lot to do with that power your motor is creating. This is important because the only part of your car touching the pavement is the tire. Owing to that fact, upgrading the tires is crucial to any performance machine.

Tire Types

Tires—also called *laces* in some tuner circles—are made for every weather condition you can think of. The main categories break down into three groups. First is the summer passenger tires, which include the various levels of performance tires such as ultra-high performance, high performance, and entry-level performance tires. This type of tire is meant for dry pavement; it won't deliver the smoothest ride, but it's intended to hug the road best when cornering and traveling at high speeds.

Laces is a slang term for tires.

Figure 19.1

Here's an example of a 3-piece wheel from HRE. Notice the rivets holding the various components together.

(Dave Reider photo)

A second category is the all-season passenger tire. These tires, although still performance-oriented, are ready to handle nature's twists, as are the ultra-high performance all-season and the performance all-season tires. The tread patterns of these tires are designed to help control water flow on the road and give your car the best traction possible in bad weather conditions while still delivering strong performance on dry pavement.

The third type is the winter passenger tire which, although meant to hug the road best in foul weather, is really not made for performance purposes. Other tire types include light truck and SUV tires, along with heavy-duty truck and SUV tires. It is important that you pick the right tire for your needs. Be sure to do your research on brands to get exactly what you want.

The Numbers Game

When reading a tire, you'll find three numbers in sequence, such as 255 45 17 or 265 40 18.

The first number stands for the width of the tire in millimeters going across from sidewall to sidewall.

The second number stands for the aspect ratio of the height of the tire (its profile) from the bead to the top of the tread. For example, a 245 40 17 will have a lower profile than a 245 50 17. The smaller the aspect ratio is, the wider the tire will be in relation to its height.

The third number is the diameter of the wheel in inches.

All three of these numbers are crucial in making the right tire decision. If any one number is not within the recommended range (see the "Wheel and Tire Plus Size Chart" Appendix in the back of this book) it may not fit properly within your wheel well, causing your tire to rub on the body or suspension parts.

Speed Ratings

The speed rating is the approved maximum speed for a specific tire. Ultra-high performance tires have higher speed ratings than standard performance tires. You can find the speed rating symbol within the number sequence of the tire size, e.g., 205 60R 15 or 245 40ZR 17.

Figure 19.3

The stretched look works well on this Volkswagen Jetta.

(Dave Reider photo)

For today's custom performance machines you're safe if you select a Z-rated tire because these tires are rated for speeds faster than your car can even achieve— sometimes upwards of 200 mph! And if you absolutely have to have the best, consider a ZR-rated tire because it's the ultimate in performance tire design.

The Right Tire for Your Ride

Deciding what tire is right for you can be difficult. The first and most important criterion to consider is the type of climate you live in. If you live in a locale where you experience all four seasons, you'll need a multi-purpose tire that can handle snow yet still give you decent performance during the summer months. Some folks have two sets of rims with two different sets of tires mounted on them. Of these, one set is mounted with all-purpose or snow tires for the winter months, while the other set is a nice set of custom rims with a set of high-performance tires on them. And the true hard-core racer may even have a third set of DOT approved drag tires on a set of lightweight rims ready for track action, too.

Figure 19.4

This Beetle exemplifies a perfect fit; notice how the wheel sits flush to the body lines—real class.

(Dave Reider photo)

Wheels

Wheels—or *shoes*, as some tuners refer to them—really have an immense impact on the overall appearance of your ride, so they deserve a lot of thought and attention when you are planning the way you want your ride to look.

TUNER TALK

Shoes is a slang term for wheels.

Wheel Construction

A commonly asked question concerning wheels is why such an enormous price range exists between brands. Many good quality wheels are available for less than $200 per wheel, while other wheels can cost several thousand dollars per wheel. The vast discrepancy in these costs comes from the different processes used to make the wheels.

Less expensive wheels are made using a process called casting. In this process, molten steel is poured into a mold to create (or cast) the wheel. When the casting is finished, the completed wheel is one large piece of metal. At that point, the manufacturer will paint, polish, or chrome it to give it the finishing touch.

More expensive wheels are made by forging. In forging, the metal is pressed, pounded, and squeezed under great pressure into high strength parts and assembled with a cast center piece using rivets. One type of wheel created using this method is the 3-piece wheel.

Figure 19.5

Check out these 20" rims and low-profile tires on this wide body Corvette; now that's an aggressive stance

(Dave Reider photo)

1-, 2-, and 3-Piece Wheels

Which way should you go when it comes to choosing wheels: 1-piece, 2-piece, or 3-piece? The first and most obvious difference is price. A 1-piece custom rim is less than half the price of a 3-piece wheel.

Many folks believe a 1-piece wheel is better structurally because it is cast and, therefore, stands less of a chance of being bent than multi-piece wheels. However, this is a wrong assumption, and here's why. With a multi-piece wheel, each piece is precisely designed for its specific job, and when the pieces are combined during assembly, the result is a wheel that's actually stronger than any cast (1-piece) wheel available. The 1-piece wheel is, just as it sounds, one solid piece; a 2-piece wheel consists of a barrel (otherwise known as the lip) and a center.

With 3-piece wheels, the barrel is actually comprised of two separate pieces, an inner section and outer section, and the center is the third piece. If you damage a 1-piece wheel, you will likely have to get an entirely new replacement wheel based on how bad it is damaged. On the other hand, if you damage a 3-piece wheel, you'll only have to replace the part which is damaged. Sounds good, right? Yes, it is, but don't let that fool you; replacing a damaged part will cost you a pretty penny, too.

Choosing the Right Wheels

Any custom car enthusiast will tell you that wheel choice is the most critical appearance aspect of your ride. Your rims will totally make or break the look of your ride. If you go with something too flashy, they'll stand out like a sore thumb; but if you go with something too subtle, they may not be noticed at all.

Figure 19.6

This Supra sits on a set of custom HRE polished shoes with some ultra-performance Pirelli laces.

(Dave Reider photo)

You have literally hundreds of wheel brands and models to choose from, and the hardest part is trying to imagine what your ride will look like with a specific rim on it. Unfortunately, no shops will let you mount rims to test fit their appearance. But take heart. As we mentioned earlier, technology often comes to the rescue and provides us with yet another great asset: virtual wheel testing. There are software programs available that let you test fit different styles of rims on different cars to get an idea of the look before making the purchase. Some specialty wheel retailers have these programs available for their customers, and many national tire/wheel retailers, such as Tire Rack, let you do these test fits right online using their websites. So definitely try to find a shop that offers this ability so you can see how your ride is going to look with the particular wheels you are considering before you part with your money.

Going Bigger

The current vogue trend is to put bigger wheels with thinner tires on tuners because this really gives them an exaggerated, aggressive look that is desired by many. As with anything else, however, you can overdo it. Remember—balance is the key!

Plus Sizing—Why Bigger Is Better

Beyond the awesome look your car will have with larger diameter wheels and wider tires, replacing your stock wheels and tires with a more aggressive package will actually increase your vehicle's stability and traction. Installing wider rims and tires puts more meat on the road, thus allowing you to hug corners better and control the car in a tighter fashion.

By increasing the width of your rim and tire package by just one inch, the result is an all-around increase of four additional inches of roadway contact. Perhaps that doesn't sound like a lot, but it will definitely give you a significant difference. Once again, everything must be done in proportion to maintain that all-important balance. You can't just go out and slap on the biggest wheel and tire package you can find; you still need to stay inside a set of parameters because each and every make and model is different. If you go too wide, you won't be able to make turns properly if at all because of tire rub on the inside of the wheel well.

Figure 19.7

This J Line 3-piece wheel fills the entire wide body. Look how deeply that barrel sits!

(Dave Reider photo)

Choosing a Larger Wheel

In today's car customizing trends, it's common for enthusiasts to increase the diameter of their wheels while using low-profile tires. Companies such as Giovanna are making rims in excess of 26" in diameter for full-size truck and SUV applications. Most of today's reputable shops have recommendation charts to help you understand what your options are. The important rule of thumb is that you have to match your new rim and tire package to the exact outer diameter of your factory package. If you do this, you will be in great shape; but if you don't, your speedometer will read incorrectly or, worse yet, you could possibly do damage to the driveline of your car, especially the transmission.

Also, with a larger diameter wheel you will be forced to use a smaller sidewall or low-profile tire. Though they give you a really cool performance look, they lessen the amount of cushioning and make your wheels more prone to injury or bending, a fairly common consequence of low-profile tire set-ups.

Going with a Wider Tire

The same caveats go for tires; you can't just purchase the coolest looking tire you see because it has a cool tread. You need to purchase tires based on the width of your rim and the clearance your wheel well provides. If you go with a wide tire in the front of your car, you want to make sure that you can maintain your complete turning radius, and in the rear be sure your new wider tire doesn't interfere with your control arms. All rim and tire shops have recommendation charts, so do your research before you make a purchase. This is really important, because once you mount a tire on a wheel, no retailer will give you a refund or exchange it for something else. When you buy it, it's yours, period. Be sure to see the "Wheel and Tire Plus Size Chart" Appendix in the back of this book.

The Least You Need to Know

- Multi-piece wheels cost more than 1-piece wheels.
- Multi-piece wheels are stronger than their single-piece counterparts.
- It's important to maintain the same outside diameter as the stock tires have when upgrading to plus size wheel/tire packages.
- Going too large on the wheel/tire combination will interfere with the steering at the front and rub the control arms and wheel well at the rear.

Part 6

Customizing the Cabin

While your ride is drop-dead gorgeous from the outside, you'll be spending the majority of your time inside it, so it only stands to reason that the interior should be as great looking as the outside, right?

But more than just attractive, it should also be comfortable and have all the goodies you want—and deserve—to make cruising in her as pleasurable as it can and should be. Stuff like soft, comfortable seats, eye-catching gauges, interior "mood" lighting, a killer sound system, navigation and video systems—how about a video game system, too, while we're at it?

It's all up to you—you can have it all, and only you know what your tastes are and what appeals to you. So step into the wonderful world of interior appointments, pick and choose what turns you on, and then, with our help, go for it!

Chapter 20

Touchy, Feely

In This Chapter

- ◆ Steering wheels, gauges, and more
- ◆ Gauging the action
- ◆ Let there be light

Your ride is really a wonderful machine, one that gives pleasure to almost all your senses. After all, it's nice to look at; it probably sounds really cool; and when you get in it, it gives you a great sensation of speed and power. But the sense that gets the most feedback from your ride is the sense of touch; after all, your body comes into contact with the door handle, steering wheel, pedals, knobs, switches, seats, and anything else you touch in the car, right? That's why we've included this chapter on things that you come into contact with while driving, so read on!

Appealing Appointments

The interior of your vehicle is where you spend time while driving, so why not give it the royal treatment, too? The nice part about modifying your interior is that interior parts are more universal than those used for the exterior or the motor. Because of this, the interior is generally easier and less expensive to modify. Many of the aftermarket components are quite versatile, and the same part number will usually fit many applications.

Figure 20.1

This is a nice, simple yet sleek aftermarket wheel from SPW.

(Dave Reider photo)

Steering Wheels

Swapping out a steering wheel is a quick and easy exchange when no airbag is involved. However, if your vehicle is equipped with an airbag, check your local laws about the consequences of removing it before you do so. In order to remove a steering wheel, you'll be wise to use a tool called a wheel puller. Though a wheel puller will definitely make life easier, it is not absolutely essential; most wheels will come off with some good old elbow grease and some persistent effort.

Figure 20.2

A steering wheel puller like this one is inexpensive and will save you lots of time and effort if you're going to swap out your stock steering wheel.

(Tom Benford photo)

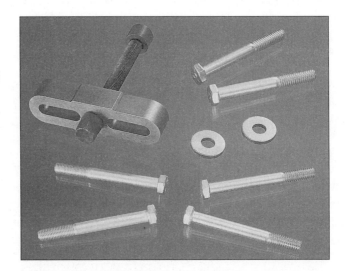

After you remove your stock wheel, you'll need to install a hub adapter made by companies such as Grant and Momo. The hub adapter connects to the steering column and provides the appropriate mounting points needed for the new wheel.

Figure 20.3

Here's an aftermarket wheel by Momo on this Ford Focus.

(Dave Reider photo)

IN THE KNOW

Hub adapters are specific to each vehicle, so be sure to check the manufacturer's application chart to get the one that's right for your car and aftermarket wheel.

Once the hub adapter is in place, you can reconnect the horn wires and install your new wheel. Dozens of companies produce steering wheels, including Grant, Sparco, and Veilside, so be sure to do your research to decide which wheel and style looks and feels best to you.

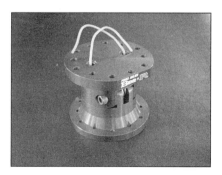

Figure 20.4

This is what a steering wheel quick disconnect looks like. Stealing a car without a steering wheel is all but impossible.

(Dave Reider photo)

IN THE KNOW

If you really want something trick, install a quick disconnect for your new steering wheel. This piece installs between the hub adapter and the steering wheel and lets you remove your new steering wheel and take it with you on the go. This is not only trick, but it is also extremely difficult to steal a car without a steering wheel!

Knobs, Switches, and Trim

Upgrading the little things makes a car stand out. Companies such as Billet Specialties make all kinds of polished or brushed *aluminum billet* replacement heating and AC control knobs, window and door lock replacement switches, and an array of trim panels such as the trim that goes around your door handle and shifter.

Figure 20.5

Illuminated interior switches and buttons come in a wide variety of styles for just about any application you can think of.

(Dave Reider photo)

TUNER TALK

Aluminum billet is produced by extruding aluminum through a die. The process of extruding aluminum has been compared to squeezing toothpaste from a tube where the paste takes the shape of the tube opening. An aluminum billet, heated to between 800 to 1000°F, is placed in the extrusion press and forced under pressure through a die. The die may contain one or more openings having the desired finished cross section. Limitations on length of parts are the result of the weight of the extrusion billet and/ or capacity of the down stream extrusion equipment. Custom automotive and motorcycle parts are frequently made of billet aluminum.

Companies such as Exotic Wood Dash make dash trim kits in all kinds of finishes. Wood, carbon fiber, and stainless steel are just a few examples; kits are available with as few as 5 pieces but can be as extensive as 30 pieces or even more. A custom dash kit is a great way to add a touch of class to any vehicle.

Figure 20.6

This Subaru has a custom billet shifter handle installed, and the leather boot is a custom aftermarket, too.

(Dave Reider photo)

Handles

Upgrading your shifter handles and emergency brake handles are easy-to-do modifications that have great eye appeal. Companies such as Momo, Veilside, and Sparco make replacement shifter handles for both automatic and manual transmissions. Making the swap merely involves removing the stock handle, which is usually held on by pressure, and installing the new one with the included hardware. Most shifter handles are universal as are the emergency brake (e-brake) handles. The most common aftermarket units usually incorporate some amount of carbon fiber for added strength. If you can match your shifter handle and e-brake handle to your pedals, you can give your interior a smooth, clean look.

> **YELLOW FLAG**
>
> It is very common for aftermarket shift handles to come loose. Put a drop of Loctite thread locker on the provided screws before tightening your new pieces down for some extra security. .

Figure 20.7

Loctite liquid thread locker comes in several formulations and is great for making sure set screws, nuts, bolts, and other fasteners don't vibrate loose.

(Tom Benford photo)

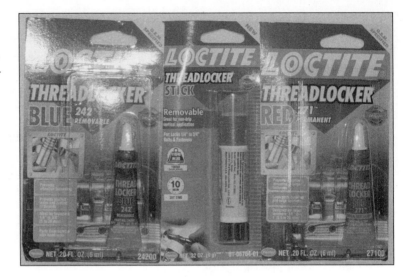

Pedals

Installing aftermarket pedals is another quick and easy customizing modification. Two types of pedal kits are available: one for automatics and one for manuals. A manual kit comes with three pieces: clutch, brake, and accelerator overlays. The automatic kit won't have the clutch pedal piece but instead will give you a wider brake pedal piece. There are hundreds of styles from dozens of manufacturers to choose from, so it's really a buyer's market here. Make sure you do your research to find the one that fits your personal taste.

Installation of a pedal kit is a pretty straight-forward matter. First, remove the rubber overlays that sit on your pedals by peeling them off; next, follow the instructions to assemble the brackets that sit behind the pedal. The new pedals are actually just covers that slip over the existing pedals and are held in place by clamps that screw in from the back side.

Gauges

You can think of gauges as "windows" to your engine because like windows, they let you see exactly what's going on under the hood with regard to temperature, oil pressure, battery condition, and more, as well as how fast you're going, how much fuel you have left, and other important stuff. So the gauges play a very important role in keeping you informed about your vehicle.

Color for Your Dash

Another popular modification is the replacement of your dash gauges. The simplest of changes is to modify the face color of your existing gauge cluster with any one of the many variations and options available from aftermarket manufacturers. The most basic mod is to install a simple colored panel; for this, you just remove the needles and lay the overlay on top. Getting a little more trick involves going to lighted units; these are overlays that change the original colors of your cluster and give your dash board a completely different look. There is some wiring and bulb replacement involved with these; however, most come with a dimming control so you can adjust the brightness and color shade to your liking.

YELLOW FLAG

Before removing the needles from your factory cluster, take note of the exact needle positions. This is extremely important because you must put the needles back on exactly the way you removed them or your gauges will not read correctly.

Figure 20.8

Stewart Warner makes these white-faced gauges for monitoring all sorts of engine functions, and they have that all-business, performance look, too.

(Dave Reider photo)

The Performance Look

Adding aftermarket gauges to your dash board can give a race theme and style to your vehicle. Installing gauges on the dash board is the easiest way to do this, but some like to be more creative. Making custom housings that replace ash trays and vents is common, especially since it's relatively easy to create gauge housing panels with fiberglass. Some folks even install gauges in their door panels and center consoles, too. It is also quite common to install gauges on the *A-pillars*. Companies such as Gauge Works make direct replacement A-pillars that can hold two or three gauges.

> **TUNER TALK**
>
> **A-pillars** are the pieces that support the windshield and separate it from the front windows.

Figure 20.9

Here's a very clean-looking gauge installation in a Volkswagen Beetle.

(Dave Reider photo)

Monitoring Your Motor

It's a common and popular mod to install an aftermarket tachometer and shift light package—not just because it's cool but also because it helps you know when you've reached the optimum shift point so you don't over rev and damage your motor. It's also popular to install an air-to-fuel meter that monitors the air-to-fuel ratio being sent into your motor so you know whether your motor is running rich or lean.

Figure 20.10

A lot of custom fiberglass work was required on this A-pillar so it could house this array of gauges.

(Dave Reider photo)

For those with superchargers or turbochargers, you definitely want to have a boost gauge to view, as you want to keep a close eye on how much boost you're making. Other popular gauges include temperature gauges to make sure components don't overheat and/or pressure gauges to confirm components, such as the fuel system, are creating the proper pressure needed.

Figure 20.11

Another very clean gauge installation, this time right in the dashboard of this Subaru.

(Dave Reider photo)

These mods are both cool and functional because it's always better to monitor your motor at all times rather than to become aware of a problem after the fact. As the old adage goes, "an ounce of prevention is worth a pound of cure." You can't head off a problem if you don't know there is one, right?

Figure 20.12

This Cavalier sports a custom-made dashboard built around the gauges; how trick is that?

(Dave Reider photo)

Keeping an Eye on the Audio System

Today's advanced car audio and video equipment is quite sophisticated—and expensive. By installing a volt meter and temperature gauge, you can monitor your equipment right from the driver's seat. You'll also want to know if you can crank up the volume some more or if you are overworking your gear and putting your equipment in danger. Don't forget that electronics get hot and need to breathe, too. When you have several amps and speakers inside your trunk, breathing can be quite limited. So by taking the time to install a few gauges in the cockpit, you can potentially save yourself from meltdowns, both equipment and financial.

Figure 20.13

Here's a great use of LEDs to put a nice, enhancing glow on the gauge cluster.

(Dave Reider photo)

Interior Lights Set the Mood

Neon and LED lighting can be a great way to accent the mods you've made inside your car. Be careful when installing neon in your cockpit, however. Balance, as always, is the key here: if you use too much, it may actually become a distraction; if you use too little, it won't be noticed.

Figure 20.14

Though you can't see a single tube, the whole trunk is bathed in glowing neon light.

(Dave Reider photo)

Neon

It is common to install neon under the dash and seats to light up the floor and/or install lighting behind items like amplifiers and speakers to give them a colored accent. Most customizers use neon to accent their modifications, and it is more common to see only the glow of the bars rather than the lights themselves. Interior neon can be a great way to attract attention to your vehicle, especially at a nighttime meet or any type of dark setting.

LEDs

LED tubes act in the same fashion as neon tubes although they give off a brighter light and last longer; they're also quite a bit more durable than neon and tolerate abusive shocks and vibrations better. The intricate builder may choose to use individual LED lights such as those made by Varad. These allow more options for installation than full tubes. Tubes, whether neon or LED, tend to be bulky and very often limit your installation options for some locations. With individual LEDs, however, you can practically locate them anywhere you want because they are smaller in size than the eraser on the end of a pencil. But be careful when handling them because individual LED lights are extremely delicate. Also, since each one has to be wired individually, installation can take quite a bit of time if you plan on using very many of them. And always be sure to take the time to get all the wiring properly run and secure.

Figure 20.15

These speakers are backlit with glowing neon rings for a really trick look. The neon can even be made to "dance" to the music with specialty controllers.

(Dave Reider photo)

Accent Lights

A simple and quick modification to any ride is to swap out the OEM interior bulbs with colored aftermarket replacements. You can replace lights such as your dome light or door lights (if your car comes equipped with them) with colors such as red, blue, green, or purple.

Figure 20.16

This strobe light looks innocuous and simple but is a real attention-grabber when it starts to flash.

(Dave Reider photo)

Another lighting modification that stands out a bit is the installation of interior strobe lights available from companies such as Street Glow and LiteGlow. These lights are great for attracting attention. Strobe lights emit a quick flash that's sure to attract the attention of anyone near by. These interior strobes come available in self-contained units so all you have to do is mount and connect them. As with most other modifications that can cause a distraction, strobes are illegal to drive with while on, so be careful and law-abiding.

Figure 20.17

The hidden neon under the dash gives the floor area a really nice glow.

(Dave Reider photo)

The Least You Need to Know

◆ Swapping the steering wheel is an easy and great modification for cars that don't have driver-side air bags.

◆ A steering wheel quick-disconnect is a terrific theft deterrent.

◆ Adding extra gauges can look trick and be very functional at the same time.

◆ Interior lighting using neon or LEDs can really change the mood and ambience inside the vehicle.

Chapter 21

Seating

In This Chapter

- ◆ Luxury and high-performance seating
- ◆ Upholstery options
- ◆ Carpeting, headliners, panels, and more

Seats—try driving your car without them. Or even try being a passenger without something to sit on. Ouch! Indeed, seats are important, not only as functional items but also when it comes to giving your ride that special interior touch. As you'll see in this chapter, seats can not only look good but can also provide just what you need when it comes to planting yourself comfortably in your ride. But there's a lot more than seats covered here (excuse the pun), so read on!

More than "Butt" Buckets

The subject of seating is definitely a controversial one. Some builders will tell you they prefer comfort and relaxation; others say swapping stock seats with racing units is the way to go. Who's right? Well, there is no right or wrong answer; it all depends on the type of enthusiast you are. Is your vehicle designed for style or performance? Answer that question, and you will know what type of seating is right for you.

TUNER TRIVIA

Today's auto parts recycling yards used to be called "bone yards" and "junk yards" in less politically-correct times.

Luxury Seats

A very common modification is to "transplant" seats from a luxury car. Taking the seats from a Lexus or Mercedes and installing them in your ride will definitely give your car a touch of class. However, there is a lot of measuring to do here. You need to make sure the seats are not too wide and don't sit too high. Unfortunately, there is no chart to tell you what is interchangeable, so finding the right seats to fit your ride can be quite a challenge.

IN THE KNOW

An auto salvage yard is a great place to find replacement seats for your ride, as well as other parts like gauges you may want to use for customizing. Additionally, you can find doors or other damaged parts that need replacing here as well.

Figure 21.1

These seats use a nice two-tone black leather and gray suede combination.

(Dave Reider photo)

After you find a seat that will work, you need to custom-fabricate seat brackets that will mate the new seats to the existing holes in the floor of your ride. For the builder who wants to go all out, consider having a professional custom create a wiring harness for you so that you can hook up luxury seat features, such as lumbar support, heat, and all the various seating adjustments. Once you take care of the mounting and any wiring, the only thing left to do is to reupholster the seats to match the rest of the fabric and color in your car.

Figure 21.2

Another nice two-tone seat, this time using black piping to set off the two colors—a real nice accent.

(Dave Reider photo)

Hi-Performance Racing Seats

Racing seats are an extremely noticeable modification to any vehicle. True racing seats are very light in weight, less than one third the weight of stock factory seats.

The weight loss is significant and so is the amount of comfort you sacrifice. You won't find any creature comforts such as seat warmers or lumbar adjustments with racing seats, and you can forget reclining seat backs and leg comfort adjustments as well. This will certainly sound disappointing to some, but those who like to go fast, spend some time at the track, and are concerned about safety will definitely make this after-market modification.

These hi-performance Status seats are covered in deep blue suede.

(Dave Reider photo)

Since racing seats are designed to hug the body, you are supposed to fit tightly in the seat. All racing seats have built-in means to accommodate racing harnesses; when you are strapped into one of these seats, your body won't feel like a maraca on a conga line in the event you do lose control of the vehicle. Racing seats are a necessary addition for any performance modifier who really pushes his vehicle to its limits.

Upholstery Options

Automotive upholstery comes is several materials including cloth, vinyl, leather, and suede. Just because your ride didn't come with leather upholstery from the factory doesn't mean you can't have it now. For those who already have leather interiors, an even higher touch of class is to replace the inserts with suede. And, if you changed your factory seat to either a luxury seat or a racing seat, the odds are pretty good the upholstery on them is not going to match the rest of your vehicle's interior. Upholstery upgrades can bring the interior of your car together and, most certainly, using some nonstandard colors and patterns can really set you apart. You do want your ride to be unique, don't you?

Figure 21.4

Here's what a stock Scion TC dash board looks like ...

(Dave Reider photo)

Figure 21.5

... and here's what a Scion TC dash looks like with a top-half dash wrap.

(Dave Reider photo)

The Look and Luxury of Leather

To replace the factory cloth seating with leather is a very simple upgrade to perform. Companies such as Katskin make replacement leather upgrades that require a bit of work to install, but anyone with some patience can do it with simple tools.

These replacement kits require the removal of the factory material and installation of the new prestitched leather covers. Since all the needle work is already done, all you do is slip the new covers on and properly attach them with *hog rings* to achieve the proper fit.

Although leather upholstery definitely gives your ride an undeniably great look, it does have some drawbacks. Leather absorbs and holds heat to a much greater extent than cloth upholstery, so during those hot summer months when you get into your car, you may really feel the heat, especially if you're wearing shorts. Some builders stay with cloth or suede over leather for this reason.

Leather seats also require more maintenance than cloth; because leather absorbs heat, it also has a tendency to dry out, which causes it to crack over time. You'll need to use special leather cleaners and treatments to boost the longevity of the material and to keep it supple. But if you have enough patience for some extra maintenance, the look and luxury of leather is definitely worth the extra work.

> **TUNER TALK**
>
> **Hog rings** are clips similar to large staples with pointed ends that you squeeze together to hold seat upholstery material securely to the seat frames. Hog ring pliers are specially designed to squeeze the hog rings together.

Carpeting, Headliners, and Interior Panels

Swapping out the carpeting in your ride can be a major eye-catching change in any car. Old, worn-out, or beat-up carpet just looks bad, plain and simple. The good news here is that you don't have to live with it; replacement carpeting by companies like ACC are quite reasonable in price. Installation isn't difficult, either, and you can accomplish it in a few hours.

The seats, sills, and center console of your vehicle will all have to be removed, but this isn't as big a chore as it sounds at first. The main thing is to be patient, remove all attachments, and label all the hardware properly for reinstallation. The replacement carpet will already be precut and prefit, so it's really just a matter of pulling out the old; spraying some carpet adhesive on the floors; putting the new rugs in; smoothing them out; and reinstalling all the sills, console, and seats in the reverse order of their removal.

Changing the material of your headliner to a suede or raw carbon matte fabric is another very popular mod. The hardest part of replacing the headliner material is removing the stock headliner. This is frequently a tricky task that requires a lot of patience since you have to be careful not to crease or bend the pieces. The headliner is all one piece, so this takes a bit of doing, hence being patient and taking your time is essential.

There are two ways to recover your interior panels. The first is to use spray-on uphol-stery dye, available from any better automotive supply store. For the absolute best results, remove the panel from the car, mask off any and all areas that you don't want to get the dye on, shake the spray can well and thoroughly, and spray the panels. As is the best practice anytime you're using a spray finish, several light coats will yield a better, more uniform finish than one heavy coat. You'll also minimize the risk of pud-dling or runs by applying light coats. While this doesn't change the material of the panel, it will change the color, and these dyes are very durable.

Figure 21.6

Here's an example of a stock door panel …

(Dave Reider photo)

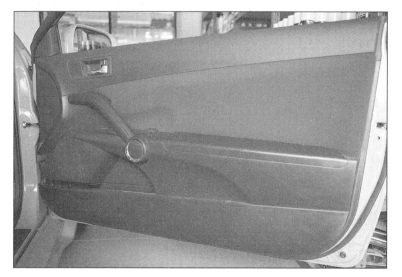

Figure 21.7

… and a door panel that's had a new insert added.

(Dave Reider photo)

IN THE KNOW

Snap-on, reusable spray can trigger grips are great for use with aerosols like interior dyes. They give you a much more comfortable grip on the spray can and also give you a lot more control of the spray itself. They only cost a couple of dollars, and they're well worth the investment. Most paint, auto supply stores, and home improvement centers stock them.

The second method for changing the look of your interior panels is to upholster them. This may be difficult, though, especially on areas that have hard plastic finishes that didn't come wrapped in upholstery material originally. Because of this, it may be a modification that you should consider contracting a professional to perform. However, if your door panels already have upholstered factory inserts, you can easily remove these inserts and change the material to leather or even suede as desired.

Figure 21.8

Carrying the theme throughout the car is important, as illustrated here. Notice how nicely the two-tone back seat matches the rear deck that's also been reupholstered.

(Dave Reider photo)

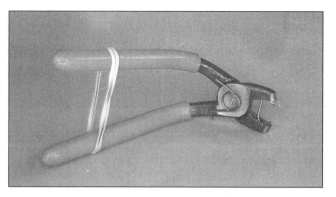

Figure 21.9

Looping a rubber band around the handles of your hog ring pliers after inserting a hog ring in the jaws, as shown here, will eliminate fumbling when you're ready to insert the hog ring into the upholstery; having the hog ring preloaded like this lets you use both hands to pull the material taut with the hog ring ready and waiting in the jaws of the pliers.

(Tom Benford photo)

Going the Suede Route

The most popular upholstery material in modern tuner circles these days is suede, a plush material that looks rich and classy. Suede is used for headliners and door inserts quite often. It is also quite popular to put suede inserts in seats, thus making them two-toned and two-textured with a leather/suede combination that positively reeks of class! And using contrasting colors that harmoniously flow with the rest of the interior can also produce a really nice look. Some companies, such as Status, have also begun to make racing seats that are completely upholstered in suede, so you have a lot of options here.

The Least You Need to Know

- Nothing beats the look of leather when it comes to seat upholstery.
- Leather requires more maintenance than cloth seating, but it's worth the extra effort.
- Interior dyes for fabric and plastics, including seating material, can be an easy and inexpensive way to change the interior color of your ride.
- Changing the headliner requires time, care, and patience.

Chapter 22

Audio and Video Gear

In This Chapter

- Getting a grip on gear
- Tunes for your tuner
- Screen choices
- It's all in the game

Just a few short years ago a multi-disc CD player was about as good as it could get in your car, but things have come a long, long way since then. Now car audio systems that can blow your doors off have become commonplace, and video systems with GPS and DVD capabilities, along with state-of-the-art videogame systems give you all the comforts—and fun—of your living room while taking it on the road. See for yourself; check out this chapter!

Sounds Good to Me

Electronics play a major role in today's aftermarket automotive industry, and that role will continue to become increasingly more important in the future. You've probably installed a surround-sound audio system with Dolby digital in your home, placing the speakers in specific locations for optimal sound to recreate the movie theater experience. Well, the same has become just as popular to do in your car. Some folks believe they spend just as much, if not more, time in their car than at home. So why not take the luxuries of home with you on your travels?

Radios/CD/MP3 Players

The first upgrade the majority of people make to their audio system is to install a higher-end radio. Stock radios are extremely limited in their options and expansion capabilities. Exchanging the factory radio for an aftermarket unit such as those available from Alpine, Eclipse, or Pioneer will give you much greater freedom to expand your system.

Figure 22.1

Upgrading to a higher-end stereo radio is a good first step. Combo units like this that can play CDs and have multiple MP3 playing capabilities are popular and inexpensive.

(Tom Benford photo)

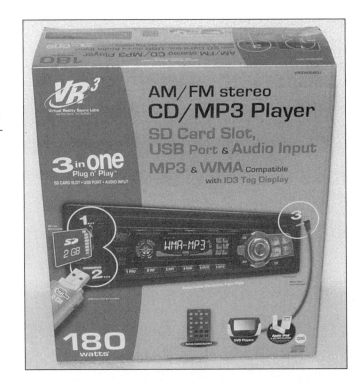

A basic upgrade would consist of a single-*din* or double-din radio that is an AM/FM receiver plus CD player. Higher-end units may consist of flip-out screens that may even be touch-screens and might also include DVD players and navigation systems.

> ### TUNER TALK
>
> **Din** refers to a standardized size (2" high x 7" wide) for automotive radios which can be installed and removed from the front of the dash, unlike the older shafted automotive radios that were nonstandardized in their sizes and had to be installed and removed from the rear of the dash. Double-din (4" high x 7" wide) is designed to fit certain automakers dash openings which utilize a larger radio or a combination of a radio and a pocket tray or, sometimes, a radio with a touch screen or other larger graphic display.

Speakers

After you upgrade your source unit, you'll most certainly want to upgrade those factory speakers as well, since the factory units are just not capable of producing very high-quality sound. With so many manufacturers producing aftermarket speakers, you won't have any problem finding speakers with the proper dimensions for your needs.

Figure 22.2

Here's a nice 6.5 and tweeter component set with crossover by Crossfire Car Audio.

(Dave Reider photo)

In the world of automotive speakers you'll find two types. The first is the coaxial, which is an all-inclusive speaker consisting of the tweeter, the mid-range, and the cross-over all in one piece. The second, which is the optimal way to go, is a set of component speakers, which consists of the tweeter and midrange as separate pieces with a separate cross-over unit. The benefit of using a component speaker set is that you can locate the tweeter away from the mid-range which gives your car better sound quality. It's most common to locate the mid-range in the stock speaker location while placing the tweeter toward the top of the door, dash, or A-pillar area. Most automotive audiophiles will run a set of components in the front of the car and a set of coaxial in the rear since the rear tends to act as a surround. However, if you choose to, nothing is stopping you from using component speakers all around.

Figure 22.3

A sweet and powerful JL subwoofer really puts punch on those low notes and gives you throbbing beats.

(Dave Reider photo)

Amps

Because your stock radio or even an aftermarket radio is limited in how much power it can provide to drive your speakers, it has become common to use external amplifiers to provide a needed power boost. The usual setup consists of two dual-channel amps or one four-channel amp to drive the front and rear coaxial or component speakers and one dual-channel amp to drive two subwoofers.

Figure 22.4

A sub amp and subwoofer from Crossfire Car Audio is shown here.

(Dave Reider photo)

Selecting the right amplifier for your ride is crucial. If you select too powerful an amp, you'll quickly blow out your speakers; if you choose too small an amp, it won't produce the needed amount of power to make your speakers perform at their best. Your speaker choice will dictate the necessary power requirements, and the outside of the box will tell you what the minimum and maximum power requirements are. Just stay within those parameters, and you'll be good to go.

Wiring Tips

When wiring audio, video, or any electronics into your car, you should always follow one common rule. First and foremost, disconnect your main battery under the hood. To do so, remove either the power or ground cable (your choice) from the battery terminal to make sure you are not working with "live" wires.

Figure 22.5

Here's a really sweet audio installation in this RX7.

(Dave Reider photo)

A second and also very important rule to installing electronics is to always connect the ground wire first. Regardless of what electronic component you are adding, make sure you get the ground connected before anything else. As long as you follow these two simple steps, you'll be in good shape. You can connect the rest of the wires at your discretion or as directed in the device's instructions.

Figure 22.6

Who says you can't put sub-woofers in your dash board?

(Dave Reider photo)

When running wires, always keep them away from moving parts that can cause pinching. Also always leave enough extra length to work with; trimming a lead too short can make connecting it extra difficult, whereas leaving some extra length makes your life a lot easier during the installation. You can always hide and tuck wires behind panels; no one will see a few inches of extra length anyway with the wiring hidden from view.

Figure 22.7

Here's a fully custom audio system. Notice all the fiberglass work that went into this hatch—real class, for sure.

(Dave Reider photo)

Beefier Batteries

The power and size of the stock battery in your vehicle is based on the power requirements needed when it was manufactured. Adding a set of fog lights or some neon—even an amp—is going to be okay on your factory battery. However, if you're running a dozen neon tubes and several amps in your vehicle, then upgrading your battery will help you feed the increased proper power requirements of these additional components.

Figure 22.8

When you have a lot of electronic equipment to power, upgrading to a beefier battery is a must. Case in point: notice all the power wires running from the positive terminal here.

(Dave Reider photo)

Companies like Optima make special deep-cycling batteries that can withstand much more abuse than the average OEM unit. Of course, they cost a bit more than OEM replacement batteries, but they're well worth the added investment.

The Screening Room

With the vast array of electronics available for car audio, you'd think it was all covered, but that's not nearly the case. Video has become a major part of automotive customizing. Companies like Eclipse, Icon, and Alpine make several TV options that provide navigation and let you watch a movie and/or play a video game, all from the same unit. Aftermarket 12-volt color LCD monitors come in an array of sizes from as small as 2.5 inches for small places such as rear view mirrors to 22" flip-down monitors that mount on the ceiling! And that leads us nicely into our next topic.

Figure 22.9

Here's an inexpensive onboard camera system. The camera (left) can mount on the license plate frame (or just about anywhere else you want it) and the 2.5" LCD monitor at the right lets you view whatever the camera sees.

(Tom Benford photo)

On-Board Cameras/Monitors

With the plethora of various size monitors available, you can install a video monitor just about anywhere you can think of in your ride. The more common locations include the back of headrests and sun visors, although all-out show cars have been known to have monitors installed in bumpers and deck lids; some builders even integrate 42" and larger plasma screens into their rides! The possibilities are endless. Cameras have made their way into vehicles, too, with back-up cameras becoming increasingly popular; people can link a camera to a monitor in the front or rear of the car for safer driving.

Figure 22.10

Can you find the camera in this photo? It's cleverly hidden in the middle of the Bowtie emblem, really trick!

(Dave Reider photo)

DVD Players

DVD players are also a great addition as a video source to any monitor. The easiest way to add a monitor and DVD player to a vehicle is to purchase an all-in-one unit that mounts in the dash board. Companies such as Eclipse have TV/DVD/navigation units available on the market that make it an all-in-one purchase.

Figure 22.11

Here's what an aftermarket flip-out/flip-up DVD deck looks like in the closed position.

(Dave Reider photo)

For those who don't want to replace their factory components, another option is to add an external DVD player; they connect right into the factory system and can be mounted under a seat or in your trunk.

Figure 22.12

Here's the same deck, now open. Notice the GPS navigation on the screen.

(Dave Reider photo)

A third and really trick setup is to purchase replacement headrests with the monitor and DVD player built in together. This is the configuration with the greatest flexibility, since each individual monitor has its own DVD player. This way, you can literally have each and every screen in your ride play something different, even all at the same time, if you want.

Figure 22.13

The glove box here makes a comfy home for this after-market add-on DVD player.

(Dave Reider photo)

Video Game Systems

But why stop with just a DVD player when you can add a video game console to your ride, as well? By adding a power converter (also known as a voltage inverter) to your car, you can convert the car's 12V DC output into standard 110V AC power and install any or all the video gaming systems you wish. This is definitely a great way to keep your kids busy on those long trips to Grandma's house or just a fun way to keep yourself occupied while at your local meet or car show.

Figure 22.14

Here's what you can do when one monitor simply just isn't enough!

(Dave Reider photo)

As a matter of fact, when you install a power converter, you can power just about any 110V AC source with it. Technically, you could even power up your notebook PC and get some work done if you need to. Ain't this modern age wonderful?

Figure 22.15

Decisions, decisions, decisions. What should I watch first?

(Dave Reider photo)

The Least You Need to Know

◆ Din and double-din are size standards for in-dash aftermarket electronic equipment like stereos and DVD players.

◆ When you increase the audio power in your ride, you should install speakers that can handle the increased power as well.

◆ Video monitors come in sizes from 2.5" all the way up to 22" and even larger, so you can fit one or more into just about any location in or on your vehicle.

◆ A power converter, also known as a voltage inverter, will enable you to use devices that require household AC power in your ride.

Part 7

Car Culture

So now that you've got a great ride, it's only natural that you want to show it off and talk it up with other folks who can really appreciate all the time, money, and effort you put into making it look and perform the way it now does. That's where "car culture" comes in.

There are scores of tuner clubs, cruise nights, and car shows you can be involved with as much or as little as you'd like. There are also lots of companies out there who will provide you with free products to showcase and help them promote your ride—some may even give you some cash to help you finance your customizing efforts!

And how about getting your ride featured in a magazine advertisement, in a TV commercial, or even in a movie! It's all possible, and it's probably a lot easier to get involved with than you ever even dreamed. And if you really want to know what your ride can do, the ultimate proving ground is the drag strip. We'll give you the full skinny on what you need to take her to the track and put her through the paces, whether it's just for a casual time trial or full-on competition racing.

Chapter 23

Social Interaction

In This Chapter

- ◆ Car club action
- ◆ Cruise nights and shows
- ◆ Sponsorship
- ◆ Your car, a star

Building your ride can, and should, be a lot of fun. But that's only the beginning. After your ride is done, you'll want to show it off without a doubt. And that's a good thing, since there are plenty of opportunities for you to do just that. And while these opportunities center around the cars, there's much more to "car culture" than just the rides. It's really a society within a society—a microcosm of like-minded people who all dig cool rides, the same music, and other interests. Essentially, what it all boils down to is the people; after all, cars can't talk to each other, right? It's the people who build the cars, who drive them, and who show them. And it's the people you'll be having fun with. This chapter will give you a broader picture on these social opportunities where you can show and enjoy your ride with other people who have the same interests as you.

SCC and Tuner Clubs

SCC and tuner car clubs are all around the place, literally, many of which you're probably unaware of. That's okay; that's probably one of the reasons you're reading this book right now—to find out more, right? Good.

Local and Regional Action

It is physically and practically impossible for us to list each and every car club, especially when it comes to SCCs and tuners, because more clubs are popping up almost every day. But what we can do is point you to the best source of information we know of and, not surprisingly, that's the Internet. The site we recommend most is www.tuner-world.com. This site has an extensive listing of car clubs, a description of each, their location, a contact, and their websites. And to make finding a club in your own particular neck of the woods easier, the site lists the clubs according to state. You simply select the state you're located in, and you'll find the clubs in that state listed alphabetically. It couldn't be easier to find a club that caters to your particular interest in your own state. How great is that?

National Organizations

Without a doubt, you should definitely check out the National Custom Car Association, as it is the world-wide official sanctioning body of the tuner show scene. Co-author Andy Goodman is the president and founder of the organization. Andy was a show competitor for more than five years when he identified the need for standardization and consistency in judging the show scene. He took on this challenge and wrote the NCCA rulebook, which the tuner industry recognizes as the official guideline for car show preparation and judging. Visit the NCCA website at www.4ncca.com where you'll find a wealth of additional information, links, and all sorts of interesting stuff about tuners and the tuner lifestyle.

Cruise Nights

Cruise nights are informal social gatherings that give car enthusiasts a chance to show off their rides and for others to enjoy looking at them. Usually sponsored by a local business such as a restaurant, bar and grill, ice cream shop, or sometimes by the municipality itself, they generally feature music and other forms of entertainment, and often have door prizes and/or trophies for participants who bring their rides to the event.

Showing Your Stuff

There is almost never an admission fee at cruise nights either for participants or spectators, so it's a great free evening of fun and social interaction. Of course, you'll want your ride to look its absolute best, so you may want to give it a wash and maybe some polish before taking it out to the cruise. Many folks actually do the detailing while they're at the cruise and enjoy answering questions and talking about their rides while working on them.

A couple of folding canvas car show chairs always come in handy for taking a load off your feet, and some folks also bring along their own refreshments, although food and beverages are usually available.

Cars and Camaraderie

As we mentioned earlier, the cars can't talk to each other or enjoy each other's company, but you and your fellow enthusiasts certainly can, and that's pretty much what it's all about in the final analysis. After all, what's the point of creating a righteous ride if you can't share it with other people who will enjoy looking at it, asking you questions about the mods you did, and sharing their own experiences about their own rides and what they did to them. That's really where it's at, isn't it?

And if you're new to the tuner scene, cruise nights are a great way to meet people, learn about clubs and upcoming car shows in your area, get advice from other owners who "have been there," and make new friends. From both authors' own personal experiences, some of the oldest and dearest friends we both have are people we met through the car hobby. These are folks we met because we had cars in common, and these friendships grew from there. And you may even meet that special someone at a cruise night; one never knows, right?

Righteous Rides and Cool Tunes

A cruise night without music is not a cruise night, period. Music is a driving force in all our lives and very much a part of the car culture scene. Just take a look at the audio systems in any tuner car if you need proof that music is a *big* part of it all. Without a doubt, music is going to be a big part of any cruise night. At any given cruise night at least one DJ will be pumping out the hot tunes to get the party going and keep it cranking at a fever pitch all night long. He will also make announcements about upcoming events, specials being offered by the sponsor or other businesses, and some

DJs will even make "dedications" upon request. The whole cruise night scene rocks—hot cars, cool music, plenty of eye candy (both with wheels and on legs), and all you have to do to be a part of it is to show up, so what are you waiting for?

Car Shows

While cruise nights are a great way to meet folks and socialize with them, they aren't competitive events. For those who yearn to put their cars up against others in a more structured, competitive environment, car shows are the answer.

Local Events

During the warmer months you'll find plenty of car shows to attend, both general shows and events specifically geared to SCCs and tuners. The local speed shop or custom car audio center is usually a great place to find out about what shows are coming up and where and when they'll be held. These shops usually have a bulletin board with flyers posted for upcoming shows. Additionally, many clubs and shops also have websites where you can find out all about the local happenings.

Regional Shows

The same sources that you use to find out about local events will often also provide information on regional events that encompass a wider area than your immediate locale, for example, the NJ-NY-PA-DE-CT region rather than just Monmouth and Ocean Counties in New Jersey. You'll also find more information on where and when regional shows and events are being held on websites, such as the NCCA website mentioned earlier.

Special Interest Events

Very often organizations, clubs, and even specialty equipment manufacturers will sponsor events for special interests. In the past, shows have focused on such worthwhile causes as The Muscular Dystrophy Association, Aids Awareness, or Conquer Cancer, with the proceeds generated from these events going directly to the sponsored cause. These are really great events to enter your car into, not only because they give you a chance to show off your ride, but you're also helping a worthy cause with your participation. Good citizenship is something we should always keep at the top of our "ideals" lists, and that includes being good citizens in the tuner car hobby as well.

National Happenings

Several national shows are held in various locations around the country on a traveling/ rotational basis so everyone gets a chance to participate in them. These national happenings include Hot Import Nights. Check out the Hot Import Nights website at www.hotimportnights.com, and find out more by clicking on the links at the National Custom Car Association (NCCA) website (www.4ncca.com).

Sponsors

Ever see a tuner with a bunch of brand-name decals on it and wonder why they're on the car? Chances are pretty good these manufacturers are sponsors of the vehicle. What does that mean, you ask? Simply put, the manufacturer has provided help in some form (proving products, assistance, or maybe even some cash) to the car owner in exchange for the publicity and exposure he or she will give the manufacturer's products installed in or on the vehicle.

The Sponsor's Role

The sponsor may provide you with free products, prototypes for testing and, in some cases, money for shows, races, or other events. In many instances, the sponsor will also help you promote your vehicle and may provide photos, flyers, or other promotional materials.

Your Obligations

Sponsors usually request that you display at least two small decals on your vehicle that can usually be color-coordinated to match your car's theme if requested. Sponsors also like to see that you actively promote their products. Attending car shows is an option, but it's highly recommended by sponsors, since they're interested in getting maximum exposure for the products they've provided you with.

How to Get Sponsored

While you can contact manufacturers directly to solicit sponsorship, this is a long, laborious, and frequently not a very fruitful method of attracting sponsors. There's a much better, faster, and more effective way of getting sponsors, and that's through www.carsponsorships.com (CS). CS is a sponsorship organization that sponsors the new and beginning builder who is looking to advance in the tuner hobby/industry. CS is more interested in the energetic event participant than the best car. The website gives you all the information you can want about sponsorships and provides an application form. Once you apply, you'll know if you've been accepted by a sponsor in as little as 24-48 hours; how's that for fast?

Runs and Events

In addition to cruise nights and car shows, you can participate in other events with your vehicle. Many of these are open to the public with any type of vehicle, while others may be genre-specific, for example, only open to tuners or sport trucks or SUVs, etc.

Fund Raisers

Generally held for charities or other nonprofit organizations, fund-raising events can range from car shows to slalom courses to "muffler rapping" contests to generate funds for various good causes.

Poker Runs

Poker runs are a great way to participate in a fund-raising event, and you get to drive your car while doing it. In a poker run, you drive along a predetermined route, stopping at five different stops along the way, and at each stop you draw one card. At the end of the run, your five-card poker hand is tallied, and the winning hand wins a prize which may be cash, a trophy, merchandise, gift certificates, or some other valuables. The great thing about a poker run is that you don't have to drive fast and the winner is determined by the cards, not by the car or your driving prowess. They're a lot of fun and—did we mention—you get to drive your ride, too. What's not to like here?

Community and Charity Events

As we mentioned earlier, being a good citizen is something we should all strive to be at all times. Often the opportunity will present itself for you and your car to participate in a positive fashion in some event that will benefit either your community, a charity or, in some cases, both. You've invested a lot of time, money, and effort in making your car a thing of beauty to behold, so when you have the opportunity to show it off and do some good in the process, you should jump on it. Frequently the community will have D.A.R.E. programs, and you can volunteer to participate in these. Often, schools will have driver education programs that may give you the opportunity to showcase your vehicle and your driving skills on a closed course or other such sponsored events to promote the public good or benefit a charity. You have a great ride, and you should also have a lot of pride, so get out there and do your part!

Making Your Car a Star

When you watch a TV commercial (other than for a specific car make or model), movie, or TV show, have you ever wondered where the producers get the cars they use for various scenes? Many people mistakenly think these vehicles are just cars that were parked on the street when the shot was being filmed, but this couldn't be further from the truth. The fact of the matter is that virtually *nothing* is left to chance when professional filming is being done, and that includes all of the vehicles in the scenes. And if you think about it for a minute or two, it's easy to envision how a shot could be rendered useless if the owner of a vehicle suddenly decided to move his car while the cameras were rolling. No, indeed, that would not be a good thing, and for that reason they hire all the vehicles. And they might hire yours, too, if you know how to go about it.

Getting Your Car on TV or in the Movies

Just as there are casting calls for actors when walk-ons, extras, or "crowd scenes" are called for, there are also casting calls for vehicles. In fact, agencies specialize in locating and placing vehicles on TV and in the movies. The easiest and fastest way to locate these agencies is to contact the Motion Picture and Film Commission for your particular state. In all probability, your state will have a website for this commission, and on it you will find a link for production services. Under production services there will be categories for automobiles, such as "antique and exotic." Under that category you'll find a listing of the agencies that locate and book cars for TV and movie production companies, so those are the ones you should contact. Usually, they'll ask you to supply a couple of photos of the car, a general description of it, and a website (if you have one) that shows more of the car and provides more details. These agencies do not charge anything for listing your car, nor do they charge you anything if they get your vehicle booked for a filming gig. The TV or movie production company pays the agency and pays you for the use of your vehicle. Sweet deal, isn't it?

Figure 23.1

This is the home page of the New Jersey Motion Picture and Film Commission website (www.njfilm.org). Your own home state may have a website similar to this.

(Tom Benford photo)

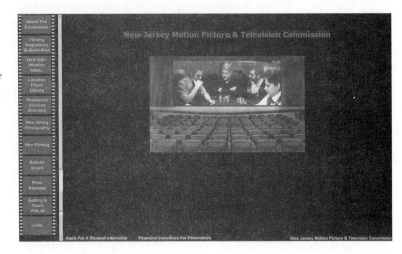

Figure 23.2

This is the production services page of the New Jersey Motion Picture and Film Commission website. Here's where all the various services for hire, including automobiles, are listed.

(Tom Benford photo)

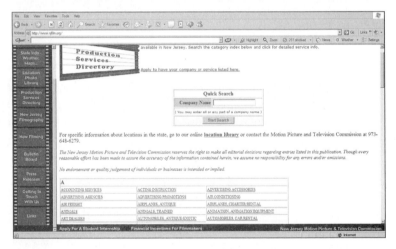

Figure 23.3

This is the "Automobiles—Antiques and Exotics" page of the NJ Motion Picture and Film Commission website. All the agencies listed on this page locate and hire vehicles for TV and movie production. Yours could be one of them!

(Tom Benford photo)

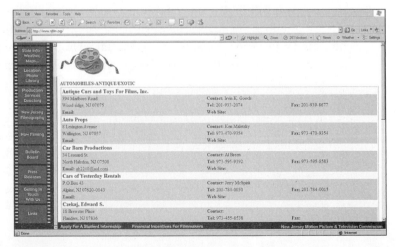

Getting It in Commercials and Advertisements

Just as no TV or movie production companies will know about your ride unless you get the word out through an agency that does this kind of placement, no advertising agency or commercial production company will call you about your car if they don't know you're out there, either.

Probably the best way to let the folks in the "ad biz" know about your car is to promote it yourself. For starters, open up the phone book to "advertising agencies," and jot down the names and addresses of all the local advertising agencies. (You can expand your contact to ad agencies further away from your immediate area later, but start with the local agencies first to see how it goes). Then take a few good color photos of your ride, and put together a flyer with your PC and inkjet printer. The flyer should show the photos of the car, describe it briefly, and give your full contact information—name, address, phone number, e-mail, and website, if you have one. Remember, they can't give you a shout if you don't give them this information.

Next, formulate a short (no longer than one page) cover letter to go with the flyer, stating that this is your custom car and it is available to hire for use in print advertisements, billboards, TV commercials, special events, and other promotional uses. Again, make sure the cover letter also has your full contact information on it. And this is *very* important—have it proofread by a couple of people to make sure the grammar and spelling are correct. You only get to make one first impression, so don't come off looking like some uneducated or illiterate jerk.

Now give each ad agency a call and explain that you have some information you would like to send them about your car. Mention that it's available for hire, and find out who the best person would be to direct your mailing to.

This phone call will serve two important purposes: 1) if the ad agency is not interested in getting your info, you won't waste any more time or a stamp sending it to them; and 2) by finding out who's in charge of making decisions about this kind of thing, you're targeting your mailing directly to the right person rather than having it filed in the waste basket if the receptionist opens it and doesn't know who to pass it along to.

Once you have all this information, put your cover letter and your flyer into an envelope, and mail it to each agency, directing it to the person in charge. Wait a week or two, then make a follow-up phone call to confirm they got your mailing and to answer any questions they may have at that time.

One of the questions you're likely to be asked is "How much do you charge for hiring your car?" This is something you should give some thought to before you make your phone calls. Decide what hourly rate you'd like to get, but be realistic. Nobody's going to pay you $100/hour to hire your car, but $200 for a half-day shoot or $350 for a full day does not seem to be unreasonable. You can also break it down by the hour, such as $50/hour with a 3-hour minimum, for example. While this doesn't sound like a lot of money, remember that you're trying to get your foot in the door here, and this first gig may lead to many more bigger and better jobs in the future, so don't be short-sighted and greedy.

Ultimately, pricing is entirely up to you. Bear in mind that if the shoot falls on a weekday, you may have to take some time off from work, so this comes into play. And don't be foolish enough to jeopardize your full-time job just to get your car into some magazine ad, so be mature about the whole thing and make decisions that work for everyone concerned. Plenty of opportunity is out there, but you're the one who has to knock on its door.

The Least You Need to Know

- ◆ Cruise nights and car shows are great ways to show off your ride, have some fun, and meet other people with similar interests.

- ◆ Always be a good citizen both in and out of your car.

- ◆ Every state has a film and television commission that provides contact information for services, such as hiring cars.

- ◆ You and your car will never get a casting call if nobody knows you're out there and available for hire.

Chapter 24

Seeing What She Can Do

In This Chapter

- ◆ Track action
- ◆ Elements of the drag strip
- ◆ Safety equipment

Okay, you've put a lot of time, elbow grease, and money into your ride making all kinds of changes to it, including some significant performance mods. Chances are pretty good that you're curious to see what all of these improvements have to do in a meaningful, controlled environment like the dragstrip. So that's what this chapter is all about—taking her to the track to see what she can do.

Taking It to the Track

The city streets are no place to test the speed and handling of your ride, and no responsible driver would do so. Aside from the fact that such immature behavior is reckless and endangers other people, a *street race* is really meaningless when you come right down to it since it doesn't give you any real, tangible, definitive proof of how fast your car really is. A legal *drag race* is the real measure of what your car can do, and there's only one place where you can put your car through its paces and have it documented, and that's at the drag strip.

> ### TUNER TALK
>
> A **street race** is exactly what the name implies: a race between two or more cars held on a public street. Street racing is not only illegal, but it is also very dangerous and highly irresponsible.
>
> A **drag race** is an all-out, straight-line acceleration run between two cars, typically over a distance of ¼ mile. An electric starting device (called a "Christmas Tree") consists of several amber lights that flash downward in sequence culminating in a green light that starts the race. If the driver starts before the green light is lit, a red light goes off and the car is automatically disqualified from the race. Many drag strips are equipped with timing lights at 60 feet and at the finish line (called traps) to record the speeds of the vehicles. The driver's initial reaction times are also measured. There is a long braking distance after the ¼ mile mark so the drivers can stop their cars safely. The NHRA (National Hot Rod Association) is the official national sanctioning body of approved drag strips throughout the country.

The Drag Strip

The drag strip is designed and constructed to allow racing to be done under the safest possible environment for both the drivers as well as the spectators. The track surface, safety walls, fences, staging lanes, and return road are arranged according to strict standards. Race procedures must conform to long established industry standards. Insurance carrier and sanctioning body guidelines must also be closely followed to ensure a safe, fair, and fun racing experience for all that attend or participate.

Figure 24.1

This illustration shows a typical drag strip configuration.

(Tom Benford illustration)

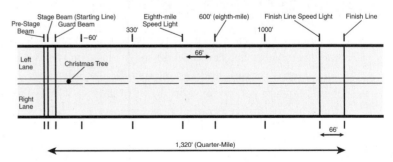

DRAG STRIP LAYOUT

A drag strip is a measured ¼-mile (1,320 feet) straight-line course where two cars race side-by-side with the goal of achieving the fastest elapsed time from start to finish.

The following components are essential to a drag strip:

◆ *Pre-stage beam:* This light beam-to-photocell connection in each lane triggers the small yellow pre-stage lights atop the Christmas Tree. The pre-stage lights signal to drivers that they are close to staging, approximately seven inches behind the starting line.

◆ *Stage beam (starting line):* This light beam-to-photocell connection controls the starting and timing of each race. It triggers an independent lane timer for *elapsed time* and will trigger the red foul light if a driver leaves too soon. A race cannot be started until both drivers are fully staged.

> **TUNER TALK**
>
> **Elapsed time**, or E.T., is the measurement of how long it takes a car to travel the measured quarter mile on a drag strip from start to finish.

◆ *Guard beam:* This light beam-to-photocell connection located 16 inches past the stage beam is used to prevent a competitor from gaining an unfair starting line advantage by blocking the stage beam with a low-installed object such as an oil pan or header collector pipe. If the guard beam is activated while the stage beam is still blocked, the red foul light is triggered on the Christmas Tree, and the offender is automatically disqualified.

◆ *Christmas Tree:* This electronic starting device between lanes on the starting line displays a calibrated-light countdown for each driver.

◆ *Interval timers:* Interval timers are part of a secondary timing system that records elapsed times, primarily for the racers' benefit, at 60, 330, 660, and 1000 feet. The eighth-mile speed light, located 66 feet before the 660-foot mark, is used to start the eighth-mile speed clocks in each lane; those timers record speed for the first half of the run.

◆ *Speed-trap and elapsed-time beams:* The first of these light beam-to-photocell connections is located 66 feet before the finish line and is used to start the speed clocks in each lane. The second beam, located at the finish line, shuts off both the elapsed-time and speed clocks in each lane and triggers the win-indicator light. The 66-foot speed trap is where speed is recorded.

Safety Gear

All NHRA-sanctioned drag strips require cars to undergo a preliminary safety check prior to doing any racing on the track. Things such as tire tread, brakes, safety belts, and steering are checked closely. No leaking fluids are allowed. Most late model vehicles with minimal modifications pass through tech inspection in only a few minutes, although some highly modified cars may require more scrutiny.

> **TUNER TRIVIA**
>
> The first speeding ticket was issued in the United States in 1902!

Roll Cages

Although a lot of builders add roll cages for looks, they serve practical purposes as well. A properly built and installed roll cage will provide the driver with vital protection in the event of a crash, especially if the vehicle rolls over onto its side or roof. Although not required by most drag strips unless the car is extremely fast (usually in the 10-second or less E.T. range), having a roll cage in your vehicle is a good idea if you intend to race it on a frequent basis.

Figure 24.2

This illustration shows a typical drag strip configuration.

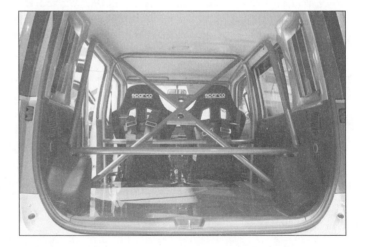

Helmets

Many drag strips require the driver to wear an approved helmet regardless of the car's speed; other drag strips impose the use of helmets for cars that are in the faster speed brackets (e.g., E.T.s of 12 seconds or less). Regardless of how fast your ride is, the use of a helmet is always a good idea at the track, and a helmet painted to match the color scheme of your ride looks cool, too.

Harnesses

Again, this requirement varies from drag strip to drag strip, but harnesses are usually required for very fast cars (e.g., E.T.s of 10 seconds or faster); however, since most late model cars are equipped with shoulder and lap belts, this may satisfy the harness requirement at many tracks.

Pushing the Envelope

Some folks find drag racing at the local strip to be an enjoyable casual activity they do occasionally; others find that the adrenaline rush they get from ripping past the traps as fast as they can is addicting and love to do it as often as they can. These folks become the hard core drivers who yearn to go ever faster and strive to push the envelope of their machine as far as it will go.

Serious Racing

Serious racing is expensive and is more than a mere pastime or hobby for many who are involved in it. With corporate sponsors and big money riding on the outcome of these races, it becomes a very serious business where nothing is left to chance, and that applies especially to safety gear.

Fire Control Systems

With major investments in these finely tuned machines, every precaution is taken to minimalize any possible damage that may occur from an unforeseen event. Fire control systems are built into the vehicle, both in the engine compartment as well as in the cockpit, to quickly extinguish any flames that may result from a malfunction or crash.

Fire Suits

Although you may not have a fire control system built into your car itself, the next best insurance to minimize injury from fire to your body is to wear a fire suit whenever you're racing. These jump suits completely cover your body, are made of flame-retardant material, and are insulated for fire protection in the event of an accident or crash. Fire retardant gloves and a mask are also usually worn under the helmet to provide additional fire protection for the driver.

Parachutes

Safely stopping a vehicle moving at extremely high speed is serious business, too. While oversized, competition brakes are usually up to the task; in extreme cases a drag chute, which is a parachute attached to the rear of the vehicle, is deployed to further slow down the car in a hurry at the end of its run.

Parachutes are not necessary for most tuners, although you will see them at the drag strip on cars that are running in the eight-second E.T. bracket.

The Least You Need to Know

◆ Street racing is illegal, irresponsible, and dangerous.

◆ A sanctioned drag strip is ¼-mile long and conforms to strict safety requirements.

◆ Every car that runs at a drag strip must undergo and pass a preliminary safety inspection.

◆ Roll cages not only look cool but are also important safety devices for serious racers.

Wheel and Tire Plus Size Chart

How to Use This Chart

"Plus sizing" is a very popular trend among customizers these days, and going with bigger wheels and tires (which is what plus sizing means) really looks cool on your ride. However, knowing how big you can go can often be confusing, so we've included this handy chart to take the guesswork out of plus sizing. Just look up the wheel and tire size your ride has as stock equipment, then check out what sizes you'll be able to go with when you plus size.

Plus Zero

Same line (this is your stock size).

Plus One

One line up and two columns right; for example, from a 16" rim to a 17" rim.

Plus Two

Two lines up and four columns right; for example, from a 16" rim to an 18" rim.

Plus Three

Three lines up and six columns right; for example, from a 16" rim to a 19" rim.

80 Series	75 Series	70 Series	65 Series	60 Series	55 Series	50 Series	45 Series	40 Series	35 Series
135	145	155	165	175	185	195	205	215	225
145	155	165	175	185	195	205	215	225	235
155	165	175	185	195	205	215	225	235	245
165	175	185	195	205	215	225	235	245	255
175	185	195	205	215	225	235	245	255	265
185	195	205	215	225	235	245	255	265	275
195	205	215	225	235	245	255	265	275	285
205	215	225	235	245	255	265	275	285	295
215	225	235	245	255	265	275	285	295	305
225	235	245	255	265	275	285	295	305	315
235	245	255	265	275	285	295	305	315	325

Appendix B

Aftermarket Product Sources

Although this is by no means an exhaustive or complete listing of every purveyor of custom components (which would take an entire book by itself), those we've listed here represent the major players in today's custom ride scene. If you have questions about any of the products or services that are not sufficiently answered on the respective websites, we encourage you to email their customer service department directly using the links on the websites.

5Zigen USA
www.5zigenusa.com
Wheel manufacturer that specializes in Japanese-brand applications.

Addco Industries Inc
www.addco.net
This company manufactures suspension components.

Bell Intercoolers
www.bellintercooler.com
Covers any intercooler need you may have.

Crossfire Car Audio
www.crossfireaudio.com
This company produces both external amplifiers and speakers.

Do-Luck
www.do-luck-use.com
Maker of high-end body kits and accessories, this company specializes in Japanese manufactured vehicles.

eBay Inc.
www.ebay.com
This is a great source for affordable aftermarket components.

Falken Tires
www.falkentire.com
This site is a terrific source for performance tires.

Ground Force Suspension
www.groundforce.com
This company manufactures complete tuned lowering suspension systems for light trucks and SUVs.

HRE Wheels
www.hrewheels.com
Makes high-end, 3-piece wheels for today's most popular vehicles.

Ignited Performance
www.ignitedperformance.com
This company makes high-quality accessory switches, starter kill switches, and HID lighting kits.

JE Pistons
www.jepistons.com
This is a great source for internal engine components.

K&N Filters
www.knfilters.com
This great one-stop air intake filter source covers everything from direct replacements to full cold air kits.

Lucas Oil
www.lucasoil.com
This company manufactures high-performance automotive lubricants.

Magnaflow
www.magnaflow.com
These exhaust specialists have applications for almost any car.

Nitrous Express
www.nitrousexpress.com
This company is the total source for all your nitrous needs.

OBX Racing Sports
www.obxracingsports.com
Imports Japanese performance products and accessories.

Pyle Audio
www.pyleaudio.com
Here you'll find great audio and video gear at affordable prices.

Quarter Master
www.racingclutches.com
This company manufactures racing clutches and driveline components.

Recaro North America
www.recaro-nao.com
This company manufactures aftermarket performance seats.

Stewart Warner Performance
www.stewartwarner.com
This is a great source for all your accessory gauge needs.

Tein
www.tein.com
Maker of high-end suspension components, they specialize in coilover packages.

Unorthodox Racing
www.unorthodoxracing.com
Manufactures aftermarket pulleys.

Veilside USA
www.veilside.com
This company is a maker of high-end body kits and accessories for Japanese-manufactured vehicles.

Wilwood
www.wilwood.com
Makes big brake kits for many of today's most popular vehicles.

Xenon
www.teamxenon.com
Manufactures urethane body kits.

Yahoo! Inc
www.yahoo.com
This provider of Internet services includes auto auctions and parts searching.

Zone Wheels
www.zonewheels.com
This company is a maker of high-end, 3-piece wheels for today's most popular vehicles.

Appendix **C**

Internet Resources

As with just about anything else, the Internet is a terrific source of information and a great way to learn about scene coverage, events, associations, teams, and other things of interest to those involved in today's tuner culture and lifestyle. Here's a good sampling of sites to get you off to a good start. You'll find hundreds of additional links on these sites, so you'll have plenty of surfing to do and no shortage of information.

Car and Model
www.carandmodel.com
This site has the latest event coverage for the hot cars and hot models.

Carsponsorships.com
www.carsponsorships.com
This sponsorship organization seeks cars and individuals to represent some of today's top brands.

DialD
www.diald.com
Online and hard copy magazine that specializes in automotive aftermarket accessories, as well as event and lifestyle coverage.

Diecast Depot
www.4diecastdepot.com
Site specializes in tuner-related die-cast cars.

Formula Drift
www.formulaD.com
This is the home of the official United States Drift Circuit.

HIN City
www.hincity.com
This online car community offers owner profiles and contests.

Hot Import Nights
www.hotimportnights.com
Largest tuner-related car show tour that visits more than fifteen cities a year.

New Image
www.newimagemotorsports.com
This show team travels cross-country with a wide variety of show vehicles.

National Custom Car Association
www.4ncca.com
This competitor body organizes the global judging and sanctioning of custom car shows.

Overboost
www.overboost.com
Here is a great source for event coverage, vehicle features, and product reviews.

Speed Options
www.speedoptions.com
This is a great source for the latest industry news.

Streettrenz Magazine
www.streettrenz.com
Online and hard copy magazine that specializes in automotive aftermarket accessories, as well as event and lifestyle coverage.

TW Competition
www.twcompetition.com
This exhibition team displays and competes with high-end luxury vehicles.

United States Custom Automotive Group Inc.
www.4uscag.com
This integrated marketing and motor sports creation corporation builds high-profile campaign vehicles.

Urban Racer
www.urbanracer.com
A lifestyle site for the performance junky.

Index

Check Out These
Best-Sellers

978-1-59257-115-4
$16.95

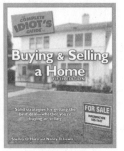

978-1-59257-458-2
$19.95

978-1-59257-451-3
$9.95

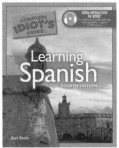

978-1-59257-485-8
$24.95

978-1-59257-480-3
$19.95

978-1-59257-469-8
$14.95

978-1-59257-439-1
$18.95

978-1-59257-483-4
$14.95

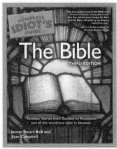

978-1-59257-389-9
$18.95

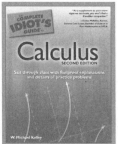

978-1-59257-471-1
$18.95

978-1-59257-437-7
$19.95

978-1-59257-463-6
$14.95

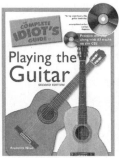

978-0-02864244-4
$21.95

978-1-59257-335-6
$19.95

978-1-59257-491-9
$19.95

More than *450 titles* available at booksellers and online retailers everywhere

www.idiotsguides.com

A
ALPHA